mexican made easy

everyday ingredients, extraordinary flavor

MARCELA VALLADOLID

Clarkson Potter/Publishers
New York

Published in the United States by Clarkson Potter/Publishers, an imprint of the
Crown Publishing Group, a division of Random House, Inc., New York.
www.crownpublishing.com
www.clarksonpotter.com

CLARKSON POTTER is a trademark and POTTER with colophon is a
registered trademark of Random House, Inc.

Library of Congress Cataloging-in-Publication Data
Valladolid, Marcela.
   Mexican made easy / Marcela Valladolid.—1st ed.
   Includes index.
   1. Cooking, Mexican.   2. Cooking—Mexico.   I. Title.
TX716.M4V334   2011
641.5972—dc22   2011004241

ISBN 978-0-307-88826-6
eISBN 978-0-307-88827-3

Printed in China

Design by Megan McLaughlin
Jacket photographs by Jennifer Martiné

10 9 8 7 6 5 4 3 2 1

First Edition

For my son, Fausto,
my biggest inspiration

contents

introduction

At 5:45 every morning, beginning when I was around three years old, I remember my mom waking up my sister, Carina, my brother, Antonio, and me so we could get ready for school, jump in the car (oftentimes with breakfast in a Tupperware container), and head for the border. We lived in Tijuana, but we went to school in San Diego. Just like thousands of other people who were going to school or work, we would wait in line, sometimes for hours, to cross into the United States. When the school bell rang, my mother would pick us up and we'd do it all over in reverse to get back to Mexico. It was like growing up in two countries—with two entirely different cultures, languages, and cuisines—at the same time.

Having a foot in each world has served as the inspiration for *Mexican Made Easy.* I grew up with all of the traditional dishes, simple to elaborate. *Tacos de adobada,* marinated pork tacos, were my favorite taco-stand find. I'd start off with cool, crunchy cucumbers doused with fresh lime juice and a little too much salt; an orange-flavored soda was mandatory. On Sundays, we'd often drive south about forty miles to Puerto Nuevo, the lobster capital of Mexico. There were so many of us that they had to put a few tables together to fit all the cousins, aunts, and uncles on my mom's side of the family. We'd feast, sometimes for an entire afternoon, on lobster, rice, refried beans, clarified butter, and homemade flour tortillas, with the sound of the *trios* playing in the background.

My aunt Martha likes to tell this story of how I learned to read at a very young age: One day when I was around four in a fancy restaurant on the U.S. side of the border—where lobster has a much heftier price tag—I told my grandfather I wanted one of those orange things with the claws on it. He said they didn't have any and that he'd take me to Puerto Nuevo next Sunday. I grabbed a menu, pointed at it, and said "Aren't they called lobsters? Because here they are." And they got me my lobster.

We're all foodies in my house; it's in our blood. My maternal grandfather, Eugenio Rodriguez, was Belgium's honorary consulate in Tijuana, which had him often traveling abroad to Europe. He'd come back with suitcases full of French cookbooks and attempt to cook from them with local ingredients. He was working on fusion cuisine way before it became trendy! The most cherished memories I have from my childhood are from the holidays spent at his house and with the food he'd prepare. Sometimes it would be traditional food, like *tamales* (page 193), *puerco en pipian* (page 86), and *flan de coco* (page 159)—and sometimes he'd whip out Beef Wellington! He's the best cook I've ever known and he passed down his love and respect for all cuisines to me.

My biggest inspiration, though, has to be his youngest daughter, my aunt Marcela Rodriguez. When she went to study cooking at the California Culinary Academy in San Francisco, I thought she was just about the coolest person in the world. Fourteen years younger than my mother, she already seemed more like a cooler older cousin than a *tía*. She earned the right to cook in my grandfather's kitchen. Like any good Mexican, she wanted to show off her family, so she would invite her cooking school instructors down to Tijuana and they'd all prepare veritable feasts. Hungry and ambitious, she soon opened up a cooking school of her own in Mexico and gave me my first job. And that's where it all began professionally for me.

It was in that little cooking school, built in the front patio of my grandparents' home, that I recorded a tape of me cooking and sent it to Food Network. Surprise, surprise, they invited me to be a guest. Eleven years later, they gave me a cooking show. The road to *Mexican Made Easy* was a long one, but those interim years were instrumental in honing my knowledge and skills to be able to share with you easier (and sometimes healthier) versions of the foods I grew up with in Mexico. You'll find dishes that have been passed down in my family from my grandparents and aunts to my mom and to me—even ones from my friends and their mothers! Trust me that these are tried and true—and delicious.

Then it's my job to make sure the recipes are simple to make for anyone, anywhere. It can be a little bit of a challenge to find the balance between easy and authentic. We have Mexican crema in San Diego but not so much in smaller American towns. But I don't want that to be a barrier to cooking up some amazing Mexican food! So I test recipes with both the traditional ingredients as well as easy-to-find substitutions to make sure the results are equally delicious. I also make an effort to create dishes that everyone knows and loves—but with Mexican flair, like mac and cheese (page 101), burgers (page 72), and lasagne (page 102), which have become staples in my house.

Then there's also the influence my son, Fausto, has in the whole process. He tests a lot of my recipes and, although he is not a picky eater at all (you can catch him eating sea urchin at the seafood market), he is *very* impatient, as most six-year-olds are. And at home it's just me and him, so it's not like someone can play ball with him while I hole up in the kitchen making dinner. (He's wise to the fact that Yogo, our twelve-year-old shihtzu, is not actually his brother, so it no longer flies when I tell him to go outside and play ball with Yogo while I finish making the enchiladas.) In other words, it's gotta be good and it's gotta be quick. And who doesn't love that?

With just two of us, we always have leftovers, so I've also become the queen of transforming yesterday's roast chicken (page 85) into tomorrow's flautas (page 28). In other recipes, you'll find ideas on what to do with extras if you happen to have any. And there's no reason ever to throw out a tortilla (unless it has turned a not-so-sexy shade of green). In fact, stale tortillas make for the best chilaquiles (page 188); because they're dry, they absorb less oil, and they stand up to the sauce better so you get a crispier texture.

I've been paying very close attention to your demands on Facebook, Twitter, and my blog, and so you'll find many of the recipes you've been asking for in this book. Here are the tricks and stories that make up my cooking life, the flavors of Mexico with ingredients you can find at your supermarket. I promise you won't need a *molcajete,* a Mexican mortar and pestle, for any of these recipes, and yet you'll still end up with some of my favorite salsas yet.

There's also the million-dollar question of how I stay healthy having grown up eating mostly Mexican food. But that's just it: I stay healthy because I'm eating *my* kind of Mexican food. My rule has been, for both me and my son's diet, to cook with the freshest ingredients possible, shooting for local and organic whenever available. The best example of this is the tortilla. I eat them every day—and a few times a day. Fausto snacks on warm tortillas spread with a little butter or a few slices of avocado and a sprinkle of salt. The important thing is that my tortillas are made solely of corn, slaked lime, and salt. And their flavor is far superior to some of those highly processed cardboard disks you find at the supermarket. So shop wisely, or make your own, which is incredibly simple to do (page 35). We're also tamale-lovers at my house. There may be a great substitution for lard (or butter, which I use for my sweeter corn tamales), but I've never found a need to adopt one. My suggestion? Have corn tamales (page 193) for lunch and a lighter dish, like Rice and Albóndiga Soup (page 57), for dinner. Moderation and balance. In this book you will find plenty of healthy dishes bursting with Mexican flavor.

But before you go off to the market to buy some ingredients and I go downstairs to the kitchen, I have just two words of advice: *Have fun!* It is only food, after all, and it just needs to taste good to you and your family. So experiment, explore, and enjoy!

Besos,

Marcela

appetizers
and small bites

there's nothing better than getting tons of flavor in a small bite. When eating with friends at home or out, I much prefer an assortment of small dishes and a chance to try an array of different flavors than one big dish. In Mexico, *antojitos*, or small bites, are fun and informal and usually packed with local flavor. Shrimp-Stuffed Little Chiles (page 22) scream of Tijuana cuisine with their mix of Asian soy sauce (very big in Baja cooking) and shrimp from the coast. I could eat an entire platter of them! And if you have never made cheese at home, you have to try it; Homemade Queso Fresco with Jalapeño and Cilantro (page 20) is so easy and super impressive to put out for guests.

So call your friends over, whip out the shot glasses (for sipping, not shooting!), get yourself some good tequila, and make a few of these recipes for a simple, memorable feast full of vibrant Mexican flavor.

chipotle-garbanzo DIP

makes ¾ cup

I LOVE HUMMUS because it's such a filling and healthy snack. You can add as little or as much chipotle as you'd like. I like to serve this with tortilla chips but feel free to put out baked pita chips or sliced raw vegetables.

1 Put the garbanzo beans, garlic, lemon juice, adobo sauce, and sesame paste in a food processor and puree until nearly smooth; the mixture will still be a little coarse. With the machine running, add the olive oil and process until well incorporated. Season to taste with salt and pepper. Transfer the dip to medium bowl. Drizzle with olive oil and a few drops of adobo sauce and top with the cilantro. (The dip can be made 1 day ahead. Cover and refrigerate, but bring to room temperature before serving.)

2 Serve the dip with tortilla chips.

1 (15.5-ounce) can garbanzo beans, rinsed and drained

2 garlic cloves, peeled

1 tablespoon fresh lemon juice

2 tablespoons adobo sauce (from canned chipotle chiles), plus more for serving

2 teaspoons sesame seed paste (tahini; see Note)

⅓ cup olive oil, plus more for serving

Salt and freshly ground black pepper

1 tablespoon chopped fresh cilantro

Tortilla chips

NOTE Look for tahini in well-stocked supermarkets in the international foods section. It's used in Middle Eastern cooking and is a key ingredient in hummus, which inspired this recipe.

queso fundido WITH CHORIZO

THIS MEXICAN VERSION OF cheese fondue is one of my favorite starters. Gooey, melted cheese is often topped with chorizo (as in this recipe), charred poblano strips, or garlicky sautéed button mushrooms and served with warm corn or flour tortillas for making soft tacos. One of my very first memories of queso fundido is eating it at a small taqueria called Cabana Suiza, in Toluca, a city north of Mexico City. I must have been five or six, and I remember vividly the delicious casseroles filled with melted cheese and yummy toppings. Plus, they had ponies and llamas outside for the kiddies to ride! Maybe I should take Fausto for a pony ride . . . in the meantime, I'll make him some queso fundido at home.

1 Preheat the oven to 425°F. Brush a 3-cup gratin or other oven-to-table baking dish with oil.

2 Sauté the chorizo in a dry medium skillet over medium-high heat until almost crisp, about 6 minutes. Using a slotted spoon, transfer the chorizo to paper towels to drain. Discard all but 2 teaspoons of fat from the skillet. Add the onion and garlic, and cook over medium-high heat until soft, about 5 minutes. Return the chorizo to the skillet and stir to combine.

3 Put 1 cup of the cheese in the gratin dish and sprinkle with half of the chorizo mixture. Top with the remaining 1 cup cheese. Bake until the cheese is almost fully melted, about 10 minutes. Top with the remaining chorizo mixture and bake for 10 minutes longer, until the cheese bubbles.

4 Serve with flour tortillas alongside for everybody to make his or her own soft tacos.

serves 4 to 6

Vegetable oil

8 ounces raw chorizo, casings removed

¼ cup chopped white onion

1 large garlic clove, minced

2 cups grated Oaxaca or mozzarella cheese

6 (6-inch) Homemade Flour Tortillas (page 35) or purchased, warmed (see page 35)

homemade queso fresco
WITH JALAPEÑO AND CILANTRO

½ gallon organic whole milk, not ultrapasteurized

¼ cup white vinegar

2 teaspoons kosher salt

2 jalapeño chiles, stemmed, seeded, and finely chopped

¼ cup chopped fresh cilantro

MAKING HOMEMADE CHEESE IS SO EASY and rewarding. Make sure you're using whole milk and that it's not ultra-pasteurized. I love adding cilantro and jalapeño for extra flavor, but you can add any fresh herb or finely diced chile you'd like. As for how to serve it, just spread a little bit over a warm corn tortilla and roll it up for a delicious snack, or impress your friends with your cheese-making abilities and serve this with crackers as an appetizer.

1 Pour the milk in a large saucepan. Heat over medium-low heat until the milk starts to simmer and a thermo-meter inserted into it registers a temperature of 195°F, about 10 minutes. Turn off heat.

2 Pour the vinegar into the milk, stirring constantly. Milk curds will start to separate and the mixture will begin to look grainy, and separate.

3 Pour the mixture into a small, cheesecloth-lined colander and let it drain over an empty pot until the curds look drier, about 1 hour. Mix in the salt, jalapeño, and cilantro. Weight down the cheese with a clean, heavy pot and refrigerate overnight (cheese will be firm). Transfer the cheese to an airtight container and discard the cheesecloth. Keep refrigerated for up to 2 days.

steamed clams WITH CHORIZO AND TEQUILA

serves 2

I SAT DOWN WITH THESE and a loaf of sourdough bread, and all of a sudden three-quarters of the loaf—which I'd been dipping into the broth—was gone! Salty-spicy chorizo, earthy tequila, sweet garlic, and tender clams make for one delicious dish. To complement those flavors, try sipping some tequila alongside. A true blue añejo agave tequila with its floral notes will enhance the flavor of the clams.

6 ounces raw chorizo, casings removed

2 tablespoons unsalted butter

1 cup chopped white onion

5 garlic cloves, minced

1 cup añejo tequila

¾ cup bottled clam juice

Salt and freshly ground black pepper

2 pounds littleneck or other small clams, scrubbed

¼ cup finely chopped fresh cilantro

1 loaf sourdough bread

1 Heat a heavy large pot over medium heat. Add the chorizo and sauté until almost crisp, about 6 minutes. Using a slotted spoon, transfer the chorizo to paper towels to drain.

2 Discard all but 2 teaspoons of the fat from the pot. Add the butter and onion, and cook over medium-high heat until the onion is soft, about 5 minutes. Add the garlic and cook for 1 minute more. Pour in the tequila and clam juice, and bring to a boil over medium-high heat, scraping up the browned bits at the bottom of the pan. Season mixture lightly to taste with salt and pepper.

3 Add the clams to the pot, cover, and reduce the heat to medium. Cook until clams open wide, 4 to 5 minutes. (Discard any clams that remain unopened after 15 minutes.) Return the chorizo to the pot and stir to combine. Divide mixture among bowls, sprinkle with chopped cilantro, and serve with the sourdough for dipping.

shrimp-stuffed
LITTLE CHILES

Vegetable oil

12 small yellow chiles

¾ cup finely chopped white onion

½ cup finely chopped red bell pepper

1 pound medium shrimp, peeled, deveined, and finely chopped

Salt and freshly ground black pepper

½ cucumber, peeled and thinly sliced

¼ red onion, thinly sliced

1 cup low-sodium soy sauce

¼ cup fresh lime juice

CHILES GÜEROS, FOUND IN MANY SUPERMARKETS across the country, are small yellow chiles, very mild in heat, with a slightly sweet flavor. Because these chiles are not very hot and because of their size, they are perfect for stuffing. I'm a fan of using sautéed shrimp, but you can easily stuff them with a marinated feta or even tuna salad. If you can't find chiles güeros, you can substitute with fresh jalapeños, but you are going to get a lot more heat, or canned pickled whole jalapeños, which are a bit milder.

1 Pour enough vegetable oil into a large heavy skillet to come ½ inch up the sides of the pan and heat to 350°F.

2 Add the chiles and fry, turning frequently, until golden brown on all sides, about 8 minutes. Transfer to paper towels to drain and set aside.

3 Discard the oil, leaving only 1 tablespoon in the skillet. Add the onion and sauté until golden brown, about 8 minutes. Add the bell pepper and sauté until soft, about 5 minutes. Add the shrimp and cook until pink and cooked through, about 8 minutes. Season the filling to taste with salt and pepper.

4 Cut a lengthwise slit in each chile and carefully scoop out the seeds, leaving the stem intact. (For milder heat, carefully cut out ribs.) Divide the shrimp filling among the chiles, then close, overlapping the sides of each opening slightly.

5 On a shallow serving platter, toss the cucumber, onion, soy sauce, and lime juice and spread out on the platter. Arrange the chiles seam side down on top and serve.

panela cheese
DRENCHED IN CHIPOTLE CREAM

serves 8 to 10

2 (12-ounce) wedges panela cheese or 2 (8-ounce) wedges mozzarella cheese

1 cup Mexican crema or sour cream

½ cup sour cream

1 teaspoon fresh lime juice

2 canned chipotle chiles in adobo with 2 tablespoons adobo sauce

2 tablespoons chopped fresh cilantro

Salt and freshly ground black pepper

Tortilla chips or pork cracklings

THIS WAS MY MOM'S GO-TO APPETIZER when we were having a carne asada. A simple mix of Mexican crema, sour cream, cilantro, lime juice, chipotles, and salt and pepper top and drench a queso panela wedge. So simple yet absolutely addictive. With either tortilla chips or chicharrones (pork cracklings), this is a perfect starter for a casual get-together. Look for a good panela cheese—nice and moist—at your Mexican market. It's also called "queso canasta" because you can see the marks of the basket that it was molded in. Really mild in flavor and favored by those watching calories because of its lower fat content, queso panela is also great for slicing and rolling up in a warm corn tortilla for a very simple taco.

1 Place a cheese wedge on each serving platter. Puree the crema, sour cream, lime juice, chipotle chiles and adobo sauce, and cilantro in a blender until smooth. Season to taste with salt and pepper. Pour the mixture over the cheese. Serve with tortilla chips or cracklings.

shrimp and avocado SALAD

serves 4

THIS IS A SIMPLE BUT ELEGANT SALAD perfect for a summer day or a champagne brunch. Make sure you find avocados that are ripe and sweet but not so much so that they are mushy or brown. A good avocado should peel as easily as a banana. If the peel won't separate from the flesh, it means it's not ripe enough (or too ripe).

1 Whisk together the mayonnaise, sour cream, chipotle chile and adobo sauce, lime juice, and ketchup in a large bowl. Season to taste with salt and pepper. Stir the bell pepper and cilantro into the dressing and then stir in the shrimp.

2 Arrange the avocado halves, rounded side down, on a platter. Fill the cavities with the shrimp salad. Serve chilled.

½ cup mayonnaise

½ cup sour cream

1 canned chipotle chile, minced, and enough adobo sauce to make 2 tablespoons total

2 tablespoons fresh lime juice

2 tablespoons ketchup

Salt and freshly ground black pepper

⅓ cup chopped red bell pepper

1 tablespoon chopped fresh cilantro

1 pound peeled cooked small shrimp

4 Hass avocados, halved, pitted, and peeled

scallop and shrimp COCKTAIL

THIS TYPE OF CLAM-TOMATO-JUICE–BASED SEAFOOD cocktail is found in *marisco,* or seafood, restaurants all over Mexico. Because of its spicy kick, it is usually thought of as a hangover cure.

1 Bring a large pot of salted water to a boil. Add the scallops and poach gently until they are translucent, about 2 minutes. Drain well and chill. Cut each scallop into quarters.

2 Stir together the cilantro, serrano, onion, lime juice, clam-tomato juice, ketchup, and hot sauce in a large bowl until well blended. Gently stir in the shrimp and scallops.

3 Divide among four 6-ounce glasses. Serve with saltines.

½ **pound jumbo sea scallops (u/15 count)**

3 **tablespoons chopped fresh cilantro**

1 **teaspoon finely chopped seeded serrano chile**

⅓ **cup finely chopped red onion**

¼ **cup fresh lime juice**

¼ **cup clam-tomato juice, such as Clamato**

¼ **cup ketchup**

1 **teaspoon bottled hot sauce**

½ **pound shelled cooked small shrimp**

Saltines or tortilla chips, for serving

chicken FLAUTAS

1 large skin-on, bone-in chicken breast half (about 8 ounces)

2 tablespoons olive oil

Salt and freshly ground pepper

Vegetable oil

6 (6-inch) corn tortillas

¼ cup Mexican crema or sour cream

½ cup shredded iceberg lettuce

3 tablespoons crumbled queso fresco or feta cheese

½ cup Grilled Corn Pico de Gallo (page 152)

A *FLAUTA* IS A FLUTE, and these addictive little tacos are so named because they resemble the musical instrument. They're easy, affordable, and delicious, and there isn't a Mexican mom out there who doesn't put these on the table at least once a week. For even more ease, substitute shredded rotisserie chicken for the chicken breast in this recipe. The fun part is putting all the toppings on the table and letting everyone build his or her own flautas. Get the kiddies to add enough fresh salsa and lettuce, and you've got a balanced meal!

1 Preheat the oven to 350°F.

2 Put the chicken breast on a baking sheet, skin side up. Brush with the olive oil and sprinkle generously with salt and pepper. Bake for 25 minutes or until cooked through. Cool slightly. Remove and discard the skin and bones. Shred the chicken with your hands.

3 In a shallow medium skillet, heat enough vegetable oil to come halfway up the sides of the pan. Lay out the tortillas on a work surface. Put about 2 tablespoons of shredded chicken down the center of each tortilla. Roll up each tortilla like a cigar and secure with a toothpick. Working in batches, fry the flautas in the oil, turning once, until golden brown on all sides, about 4 minutes. Transfer to paper towels to drain.

4 Place 3 flautas on each plate. Drizzle with crema and top with shredded iceberg lettuce, the queso fresco, and the pico de gallo.

skirt steak QUESADILLAS

serves 4

IN MEXICO, THESE ARE KNOWN AS *MULITAS*, or small mules, and I was obsessed with them during my teenage years. In high school, whenever I got in an argument with my boyfriend, he'd take me to the Taqueria Hipodromo, a Tijuana taqueria that has been there for decades, because he knew that would get me in a better mood. These quesadilla-taco hybrids look kind of like a sandwich, but one made with tortillas, of course. Most Mexicans scoff at the idea of putting chicken in a quesadilla—that only happens on this side of the border—but steak and pork are favorites. For some girls, it takes a dozen roses and a box of chocolates. For me, a good *mulita* with a perfect carne asada-to-cheese ratio, and I'm hooked.

1 Put the steak in a shallow glass dish. Sprinkle the steak on both sides with salt and pepper. Let stand for at least 15 minutes and up to 1 hour, turning occasionally.

2 Heat the oil in a large heavy skillet over high heat. Add the steak and cook, turning once, to desired doneness, about 6 minutes for rare. Transfer to a cutting board and let rest for 5 minutes before thinly slicing against the grain.

3 Heat a heavy large skillet over medium-high heat. Add 2 tortillas and warm slightly, about 30 seconds. Top each with ½ cup of the cheese, then top with a second tortilla. Cook, turning once, until the cheese melts, about 5 minutes. Open them up and add some of the sliced meat and avocado slices. Transfer to a cutting board. Repeat with remaining tortillas, cheese, meat, and avocado. Slice each quesadilla into four triangles. Serve with lime wedges and Tomatillo and Chile de Árbol Salsa.

1 skirt steak, about 2 pounds

Salt and freshly ground black pepper

3 tablespoons vegetable oil

2 cups shredded mozzarella cheese

8 (8-inch) Homemade Flour Tortillas (page 35) or purchased, warmed (see page 35)

2 Hass avocados, halved, pitted, peeled, and sliced

2 limes, cut into wedges

Tomatillo and Chile de Árbol Salsa (page 147)

tacos
and tortas

there's gourmet food in Mexico—
the fancy complex moles and salsas—and then there is
the street food that warms the soul. I lived off tacos and
tortas, or sandwiches, when I was a teenager in Tijuana.
Some of my best memories from growing up are of hitting
a particular taco stand with my girlfriends or looking for a
torta for dinner with my dad.

Tacos and tortas are so easy to prepare, so satisfying, and
scream of Mexican tradition. Almost anything can be used
to stuff them. In fact, one of my new favorites is Angel Hair
Pasta Tacos (page 39)—spicy tomato-drenched pasta
stuffed in a soft corn tortilla and then drizzled with Mexican
crema. That's right: full carb-on-carb and positively
delicious! So let these recipes be the starting point in
terms of inspiration for creating your own crave-worthy
creations at home. Warm up a tortilla and start making
your own memories!

homemade FLOUR TORTILLAS

makes 12 (8-inch) tortillas

I ABSOLUTELY LOVE FLOUR TORTILLAS WARM OFF THE BURNER, smeared with butter and rolled up like a cigar. They are incredibly easy to make and so different from the rubbery varieties you find at most supermarkets. Yes, I use lard. You have to in order to get the proper texture and flavor of an authentic flour tortilla. Honestly, I'll take a little lard over the twenty chemicals and ingredients I can't pronounce in some store-bought tortillas any day of the week!

3½ cups all-purpose flour, plus more for kneading

¾ cup lard or trans-fat–free vegetable shortening

2 teaspoons salt

1 cup lukewarm water

NOTE To warm tortillas, heat them directly over a gas burner or in a dry skillet over medium heat, turning once, for 20 seconds.

1 Using a wooden spoon, blend the flour and lard in a large bowl until the mixture resembles fine meal. In a small bowl, mix the salt and water. Gradually add the water to the flour mixture, stirring with the wooden spoon until the liquid is incorporated. Form the dough into a ball and knead it on a lightly floured surface for 2 to 3 minutes, or until smooth. Divide the dough into 12 equal pieces and roll each piece into a ball.

2 Heat a griddle over moderately high heat until hot. Roll one of the balls of dough into a 7-inch round. Cook on the griddle, turning twice, for 1 to 1½ minutes, or until puffed and golden on both sides. Wrap the tortilla in a kitchen towel to keep warm. Repeat with the remaining dough, stacking and enclosing the tortillas in the towel. (The tortillas may be made 1 day in advance and kept refrigerated in a plastic bag. Reheat before using.)

leftovers?

easy buñuelos: Fry tortillas in vegetable oil until golden and sprinkle with cinnamon and sugar while hot.

flour tortilla chips: Cut into wedges and bake at 375°F for 20 minutes, or until golden brown, for the perfect accompaniment to any dip.

tortilla pizzas: Top tortillas with tomato sauce, Oaxaca or mozzarella cheese, and prosciutto. Bake at 350°F until the cheese is melted and golden.

SLOW-COOKED carnitas tacos

½ cup lard or trans-fat–free vegetable shortening

2 pounds pork butt, cut into 2-inch cubes (4 cups)

Salt and freshly ground black pepper

4 black peppercorns

2 bay leaves

2 medium white onions

4 garlic cloves, peeled

12 (6-inch) corn tortillas, warmed (see page 35)

Salsa Asada (page 148) or purchased salsa

½ cup chopped fresh cilantro

URUAPAN, A CITY IN THE CENTRAL PART OF MICHOACÁN, is famous for its pork carnitas—so much so that it is also the name of one of the most popular carnitas restaurants in Tijuana. Traditionally, pork is cooked in lard in large copper pots (prized for their even heat conductivity) until it's melt-in-your-mouth tender. At this particular restaurant, I would sit at a large communal wooden table, with the carnitas and all their toppings in the center. I'd always order an orange soda, but for the grownups there's nothing like an ice-cold beer with the carnitas. For this recipe, you don't need the copper pot or to be watching over the cooking process. Just pop the seared pork in the slow cooker and let it go.

1 Melt the lard in a heavy large skillet over medium-high heat. Sprinkle the pork all over with salt and pepper and add to the pan. Sear the meat on all sides, turning occasionally, until golden brown, about 10 minutes. Transfer the meat and juices to the insert of a slow cooker along with ½ tablespoon salt, the peppercorns, and bay leaves. Quarter one of the onions and add to the slow cooker with the garlic cloves. Cover the slow cooker and cook on high until the meat is very tender and falling apart, about 3½ hours.

2 Using a slotted spoon, transfer the pork to a cutting board. Discard the onion and garlic. Cool slightly. Using your fingers, shred the pork. Transfer the carnitas to a platter.

3 Slice the remaining onion. Serve the carnitas with warm tortillas, the salsa, sliced onion, and cilantro for making soft tacos.

leftovers?

beans and carnitas: Chop the carnitas and reheat with rinsed and drained canned black beans and 1 whole serrano chile. Mix with fresh cilantro and serve in individual soup bowls.

carnitas volcano: Crisp corn tortillas on a baking sheet in a 400°F preheated oven for 15 minutes. Sprinkle each tortilla with shredded Oaxara or mozzarella cheese and cook until the cheese is completely melted. Top each with carnitas and serve with fresh salsa.

angel hair pasta TACOS

IN MEXICO CITY, you can find *fideo* tacos in almost any taqueria. A thin pasta very similar to angel hair, *fideos* are usually broken up and then either cooked and served in a soup or prepared *seco,* or dry, very much like a rice pilaf, as in this recipe. I sauté the pasta in a little oil, then add a tomato-based sauce and cook until it's absorbed. To add some protein to this carb-inside-a-carb dish, just stir some shredded cooked chicken into the pasta before you make the tacos.

1 Heat 2 tablespoons of the vegetable oil in a heavy large skillet over medium heat. Add the pasta and sauté until golden brown, about 6 minutes.

2 Puree the tomatoes, onion, and 2 teaspoons salt in a blender until smooth. Add to the pasta in the skillet and cook over low heat until the pasta is tender, about 12 minutes. Season with salt and pepper.

3 Fill the tortillas with the pasta, drizzle with crema, and sprinkle with cheese.

serves 10

3 tablespoons vegetable oil

1 (12-ounce) box angel hair pasta, cut with scissors into 1-inch pieces

3 large tomatoes, cored and peeled

¼ cup roughly chopped white onion

Salt and freshly ground pepper

12 (6-inch) corn tortillas, warmed (see page 35)

¼ cup Mexican crema or sour cream

½ cup crumbled queso fresco or feta

BRAISED MARINATED skirt
steak burritos

SKIRT STEAK

¼ cup fresh lime juice

2 tablespoons Maggi seasoning sauce (see Note), or 1 tablespoon soy sauce plus 1 tablespoon Worcestershire sauce

2 tablespoons water

3 garlic cloves, minced

1 serrano chile, stemmed, seeded, and minced

Salt and freshly ground black pepper

½ cup plus 3 tablespoons olive oil

1 (2- to 3-pound) skirt steak, trimmed and cut into 3 large pieces

NOTE Maggi sauce is a popular seasoning in Mexico that can be found in most supermarkets and in Latin markets.

A *BURRITO* IS A SMALL DONKEY AND, as the story goes, there once was a man who would sell his wife's *guisados,* or meat fillings, wrapped in tortillas, hot off his cart, which was pulled by a burrito. He was known as "*él del burrito*" and the name kind of stuck. Burritos in Mexico are so different from what you see in fast-food places here in the United States. They are much more slender and usually filled with just one or two ingredients, such as beans, cheese, or shredded beef, as in this recipe. I love pairing them with some pickled jalapeños and refried beans.

1 To marinate the skirt steak, combine the lime juice, Maggi sauce, water, garlic, and serrano in a medium bowl. Season to taste with salt and pepper. Slowly add ½ cup of the olive oil, whisking constantly. Add the beef to the marinade, turning to coat. Pour the meat and marinade into a 1-quart freezer bag. Seal and refrigerate for at least 8 hours or preferably overnight.

2 Allow the meat to come to room temperature before cooking, about 30 minutes. Remove the meat from the marinade and pat dry with paper towels. Discard the marinade.

3 In a large heavy pot, heat the remaining 3 tablespoons oil over medium-high heat. Sear the meat until browned all over, about 4 minutes per side. Transfer the browned meat to a platter and set aside.

4 To braise the meat, add the onion, bell pepper, garlic, and serranos to the pot. Sauté over medium-high heat until crisp-tender, about 5 minutes. Add the beef broth, tomatoes and juice, and oregano. Mix well, then return the meat to the pan. Bring to a boil, reduce the heat, cover, and simmer until the meat is very tender, about 2 hours.

5 Using a slotted spoon, transfer the meat to a cutting board and let sit until cool enough to handle, about 15 minutes. Continue to cook the onion mixture until most of the liquid has evaporated, about 10 minutes more.

6 Shred the meat into 2-inch-long pieces. Return the shredded meat to the pot, stir to combine, and cook until meat is hot, about 3 minutes.

7 Put about 2 tablespoons of the meat mixture into the center of each tortilla, and roll into a thin burrito. Arrange the burritos on a serving platter and garnish with lime wedges.

BRAISING LIQUID

1½ cups diced white onion

1 cup diced red bell pepper

3 garlic cloves, minced

2 serrano chiles, stemmed, seeded, and minced

1 cup beef broth

1 (14.5-ounce) can diced tomatoes with juice

½ teaspoon dried oregano

12 (8-inch) Homemade Flour Tortillas (page 35) or purchased, warmed (see page 35)

Lime wedges, for serving

turkey picadillo TACOS

serves 4 to 6

2 tablespoons vegetable oil

⅓ cup finely chopped white
onion

¼ cup finely chopped celery

¼ cup finely chopped carrot

1 cup fresh corn kernels (from
about 1 ear of corn) or thawed
frozen

2 garlic cloves, minced

2 jalapeño chiles, stemmed,
seeded, and finely chopped

1 pound ground turkey

1¼ cups canned tomato puree

1 bay leaf

2 fresh thyme sprigs

2 fresh oregano sprigs

6 (6-inch) corn tortillas,
warmed (see page 35)

Pickled jalapeños

PICADILLO—GROUND MEAT cooked with finely chopped vegetables and tomato puree—was a weeknight staple in my house, and we'd eat it on pretty much anything. I'd sandwich it between toasted white bread or stuff some in a warm pita with some shredded lettuce, sour cream, and pickled jalapeños. We would even eat it like a sloppy joe inside a burger bun! This simple sauté is also a favorite with kids.

1 Heat the vegetable oil in a large saucepan over medium-high heat. Add the onion and celery and cook until translucent, about 5 minutes. Add the carrot, corn, garlic, and jalapeños and cook for 5 minutes. Add the ground turkey and sauté until cooked through, about 8 minutes more.

2 Pour in the tomato puree. Add the bay leaf, thyme, and oregano and stir to incorporate. Cover, reduce the heat to medium, and cook for 10 minutes.

3 Spoon ¼ cup of picadillo onto each warm tortilla. Serve with pickled jalapeños.

leftovers?

healthy lasagna: Layer picadillo between lasagna sheets, top with cheese and Mexican crema or sour cream, and bake until golden brown.

picadillo pot pie: Spoon picadillo into a 9-inch deep-dish glass pie dish. Top with purchased pie crust and seal the dough edges to the rim of the dish. Using a small paring knife, cut several slits in the pie crust. Bake at 350°F until the crust is golden brown and the juices are bubbling thickly, about 20 minutes.

picadillo sliders: Fill sesame hamburger buns with warmed picadillo. Top with sliced avocado and pickled jalapeños.

picadillo empanadas: Fill uncooked flour tortillas with some picadillo. Enclose the filling by brushing the edges of the tortillas with egg wash and pressing together with a fork. Fry in 350°F vegetable oil until golden brown.

taco LIGHT

serves 6 to 8

OKAY, SO TECHNICALLY IT'S NOT A TACO because filling is not enclosed in a tortilla, but it sure looks like a taco—and it's delicious. It's like an Asian lettuce wrap but with Mexican fillings. I will not now (or ever) try to convince you not to use a tortilla. This just happens to be a really yummy dish that's hearty and balanced, and you don't really miss the tortilla. A great marinade makes for a truly flavorful piece of meat.

1 orange, thinly sliced with peel

½ medium onion, thinly sliced

4 garlic cloves, halved and smashed

1 flank steak, about 2¼ pounds

Salt and freshly ground black pepper

1 cup light-colored beer, preferably a lager

⅓ cup soy sauce

2 tablespoons fresh lime juice

1 teaspoon minced seeded serrano chile

1 scallion, white and pale green parts only, thinly sliced

2 teaspoons chopped fresh cilantro

1 head butter lettuce, leaves separated

1 Hass avocado, peeled, pitted, and thinly sliced

1 Scatter half of the orange slices, half of the onion slices, and half of the garlic pieces on the bottom of a 9 × 13-inch glass baking dish. Sprinkle the flank steak all over with salt and pepper and place in the baking dish. Scatter the remaining orange, onion, and garlic slicer over the flank steak and pour the beer over. Cover with plastic wrap and refrigerate for 1 hour or overnight.

2 Heat a grill to medium-high. Remove the meat from the refrigerator and let come to room temperature.

3 Remove the meat from the marinade and pat dry; discard the marinade. Grill the steak to desired doneness, about 4 minutes per side for medium-rare.

4 Meanwhile, mix the soy sauce, lime juice, serrano, scallion, and cilantro in a small bowl.

5 Transfer the grilled flank steak to a cutting board, let rest for 5 minutes, and then cut crosswise into ¾-inch-thick strips. Make tacos using the lettuce leaves as wrappers and filling them with flank steak and avocado and drizzling with the soy sauce mixture.

pork and salsa TORTAS

serves 4 to 6

3 tablespoons vegetable oil

6 tablespoons lard or trans-fat–free vegetable shortening

2 pounds boneless pork butt, cut into 2-inch cubes (4 cups)

Salt and freshly ground pepper

3 cups water

1 medium white onion, quartered

1 bay leaf

2 garlic cloves, peeled

4 black peppercorns

1 (15-ounce) can refried pinto beans, preferably organic

6 bolillo rolls (see Note), or 1½ baguettes, cut into 6 pieces

3 cups Spicy Tomato Broth (page 153)

NOTE Bolillos are oblong individual rolls. Stale ones are perfect for these sandwiches because they soak up all great the tomato broth.

SPANISH FOR "DROWNED MEXICAN-STYLE SANDWICHES," these *tortas ahogadas* were born in Jalisco, Guadalajara. The bread can be either partially or totally submerged in the sauce. The trick is to let it soak for a couple of minutes so it absorbs the sauce and softens up a bit but not so much that it gets soggy. Usually not something people make at home, this is a great dish to get the feel of Mexican street food.

1 In a large heavy skillet, heat the oil and lard over medium-high heat. Sprinkle the pork all over with salt and pepper. Sear the meat on all sides until golden brown, about 5 minutes per side.

2 Carefully add the water, onion, bay leaf, garlic, and peppercorns. Bring to a boil, cover, reduce the heat to medium-low, and simmer for 25 minutes, or until the meat is tender. Uncover and continue to cook until liquid evaporates, about 30 minutes.

3 Meanwhile, warm the refried beans in the microwave or in a saucepan over low heat.

4 Transfer the meat to a cutting board; discard the onion, garlic, bay leaf, and peppercorns. Thinly slice the pieces of pork.

5 Cut each bolillo in half lengthwise, spread 2 tablespoons of refried beans on each bottom half, and top with ¼ cup pork. Put the other bolillo half on top. Serve in shallow bowls and drench each torta with warm tomato broth.

shredded chicken IN
PEANUT-SAUCE TACOS

serves 4 to 6

MY ASSISTANT VALERIA'S MOM, MARIA ELENA, doesn't cook much. In fact, her repertoire consists of five dishes, this being one of them. The first time I made this *encacahuatado,* or "peanuty" recipe, Fausto and I had a big serving for lunch. Then I got up at midnight to finish off the rest because I couldn't stop thinking about it. There are many peanut-based sauces and salsas in Mexican cooking, but this one will quickly become one of your favorites. The incredibly simple and delicious recipe is definitely a keeper.

1 Puree the tomatoes, peanuts, peanut butter, and adobo sauce in a blender until smooth. Season with salt and pepper.

2 Pour the sauce into a medium skillet and add the chicken. Stir for 3 minutes over medium heat until warm. Transfer to a platter and sprinkle with the sesame seeds, if desired. Serve with warm corn tortillas.

2 large tomatoes, cored and peeled

2 cups roasted unsalted peanuts

1 tablespoon peanut butter

2 tablespoons adobo sauce (from canned chipotle chiles)

Salt and freshly ground pepper

2 cups shredded cooked chicken breast

Sesame seeds (optional)

6 (6-inch) corn tortillas, warmed (see page 35)

torta DE MILANESA

serves 4

4 (4-ounce) chicken or beef cutlets (each ¼ inch thick)

Salt and freshly ground black pepper

1 cup all-purpose flour

2 large eggs

1 cup plain dry bread crumbs

Vegetable oil, for frying

4 bolillo rolls (see Note, page 46), or 1 baguette, cut into 4 pieces

Easy Chipotle Mayo (page 141)

4 iceberg lettuce leaves

8 (¼-inch-thick) tomato slices

12 (¼-inch-thick) avocado slices

12 thin white onion slices

12 pickled jalapeño slices or 4 canned chipotle chiles in adobo sauce

8 lime wedges

TORTAS DE MILANESA WERE OFTEN the afterschool *comida* for my sister, Carina, my brother, Antonio, and myself. Milanesa, just like it sounds, comes from the Italian *milanese* and is identical in the sense that it's a thinly pounded, breaded, and pan-fried cut of meat. The technique, brought over by European immigrants, was taken and incorporated into one very Mexican dish, the torta. These sandwiches, made with crusty bolillo rolls, can be stuffed with just about anything you can imagine. My mom would put these on the table with pickled jalapeños and canned chipotles in adobo. Sometimes she would make me one for lunch and I'd smash Doritos between the bread and the meat for some extra crunch.

1 Sprinkle the cutlets all over with salt and pepper. Put the flour on a plate and season with salt and pepper. Lightly beat the eggs in a shallow bowl. Put the bread crumbs on a plate. Dip the cutlets on both sides into the flour, then into the eggs, and finally into the bread crumbs, pressing down on both sides so that the bread crumbs adhere to the meat.

2 Pour enough oil into a large skillet to come ⅓ inch up the sides of the pan. Heat to 350°F. Working in two batches, pan-fry the cutlets until golden, about 2 minutes per side. Using a slotted spoon, transfer to paper towels to drain.

3 To assemble the sandwiches, halve the rolls horizontally. Pull out the soft center of the rolls and discard. Spread each roll evenly with the chipotle mayonnaise. Layer on the cutlets and top with lettuce, tomato, avocado, onion, and pickled jalapeño. Top with remaining halves of the rolls. Arrange the sandwiches on serving plates and garnish with lime wedges.

carne asada cheese TACOS

serves 4

¼ cup añejo tequila

4 tablespoons (½ stick) unsalted butter, melted

2 tablespoons chopped fresh cilantro

1 tablespoon fresh thyme, chopped

2 garlic cloves, finely chopped

1 serrano chile, stemmed and finely chopped

1 pound skirt steak

Salt and freshly ground black pepper

Olive oil

3 cups shredded Monterey jack cheese

2 avocados, halved, pitted, and sliced

1 cup Grilled Corn Pico de Gallo (page 152) or purchased salsa or hot sauce, to taste

EVERY SINGLE TIME I GO TO MEXICO CITY I have to go to El Farolito, a well-known taqueria that serves some of the best tacos in the city—and that's really saying something! My meal always starts with freshly squeezed tangerine juice, some grilled onions, and a batch of guacamole served with *chicharrones*, aka fried pork rinds, lime wedges, and an array of salsas. Then I order my all-time-favorite *costras*, or crusts, which are made from melted cheese and then filled with all sorts of savory ingredients like marinated steak, adobo chicken, rajas, and much more. The crusty cheese takes the place of the tortilla in these tacos, making them unique and absolutely gratifying. In this recipe, I opt for a steak filling that gets marinated in tequila, aromatic thyme and cilantro for freshness, and a serrano chile and some garlic for a little kick.

1 In a 9 × 13-inch glass baking dish, combine the tequila, butter, cilantro, thyme, garlic, and serrano and mix well. Add the steak to the marinade, turn to coat, and season with salt and pepper on both sides. Let stand at room temperature for 30 minutes or in the refrigerator for up to 2 hours.

2 Heat a large griddle or skillet over medium-high heat and brush with olive oil. Cook the steak, turning occasionally, for 6 to 8 minutes per side for medium-rare. Let rest on a plate, covered with aluminum foil, for 10 minutes. Cut meat against the grain into ½-inch slices.

3 To make the cheese tacos, heat the same griddle or skillet you used to cook the steak over medium-high heat. Spoon 3 mounds, each using ¼ cup of cheese, at least 2 inches apart on the griddle. Cook for 3 minutes. The cheese mounds will spread flat like tortillas; make sure they don't stick together. After the cheese browns on the bottom (it will stay white on the top), add some sliced meat over half of each cheese tortilla and fold the other half over to make a half-moon-shaped taco. Transfer to a baking sheet and cover with aluminum foil to keep warm. Repeat the procedure with the remaining cheese and steak.

4 Serve the cheese tacos topped with sliced avocado and salsa.

soups

my dad used to say he could eat soup at every meal, and I have to say I see his point. There's nothing like a warm bowl of hearty Rice and Albóndiga soup (page 57) on a cold winter day or some Spicy Shrimp Broth (page 67) after a night of serious dancing and partying (it's believed to cure hangovers!). Growing up, I remember there was always a batch of Shredded Brisket in Broth (page 60) that my brother, my sister, and I would help ourselves to when we were hungry after school. Creamy Pinto Bean Soup (page 61) had to be made almost daily for my sister, Carina, because aside from dessert, it was one of the few things she would eat!

Soups are easy, comforting, and best of all, ideal to make ahead. So double up on batches, because once your family gets a taste of Tortilla Soup (page 62), they'll be clamoring for seconds.

lentil and chorizo SOUP

serves 4

SO HEARTY AND FULL OF FLAVOR, this perfect-for-winter soup pairs salty, spicy chorizo with earthy lentils. My mom used to make this all the time when I was a kid. For a tart, cool kick, I would add a dollop of Mexican crema (or sour cream) and stir it into the lentils. It lightens up the mix and makes the soup so rich and creamy!

4 cups water

1 cup green lentils

2 whole garlic cloves, peeled

6 ounces raw chorizo, casing removed

½ cup chopped white onion

1 cup cubed 1 inch peeled carrot

½ cup tomato sauce

Salt and freshly ground black pepper

1   Combine the water, lentils, and garlic in a 2-quart saucepan. Bring to a boil over medium-high heat. Reduce the heat to low, cover, and simmer until the lentils are tender, about 35 minutes.

2   Meanwhile, heat a medium pot over high heat. Add the chorizo and cook, breaking it up with the back of a spoon, until fragrant and almost cooked through, about 8 minutes. Add the onion and carrot, and sauté until the onion is translucent, about 6 minutes. Add the tomato sauce and season with salt and pepper.

3   Add the chorizo mixture to the lentils and stir to combine. Simmer over medium-low heat for 5 minutes.

4   Season with the soup with salt and pepper before ladling into bowls.

rice and albóndiga SOUP

serves 6 to 8

A ONE-DISH MEAL complete with protein, carbs, and veggies in every bite. When you have a son like mine, who can sit at the table for approximately fifteen minutes before looking for excuses to get up ("I need more water," "I need to go to the bathroom," "I need to go climb a tree"), a dish like this really hits the spot. Delicious, nutritious, easy, and spoon-friendly, it's a mom's BFF.

2 tablespoons vegetable oil

½ small white onion, finely chopped

2 tablespoons chopped fresh parsley

Salt and freshly ground black pepper

⅓ cup long-grain rice

1 pound ground sirloin

1 medium carrot, sliced

1 serrano chile

2 tablespoons tomato paste

8 cups vegetable broth

1 large Yukon Gold potato, peeled and diced

2 small zucchini, diced

1 In a large heavy pot, heat 1 tablespoon of the vegetable oil over medium-high heat. Add the onion and sauté until translucent, about 5 minutes. Add the parsley and cook for 1 minute. Season with salt and pepper. Let cool slightly.

2 Mix the rice, ground meat, 2 teaspoons salt, and ½ teaspoon pepper in a large bowl. Add the sautéed onion mixture and mix until incorporated. Using wet hands, shape into 20 meatballs, each about 1 inch in diameter.

3 Add the remaining 1 tablespoon oil to the same pot and sauté the carrot and serrano for 5 minutes. Mix in the tomato paste and vegetable stock, and bring to a boil. Add the meatballs, potato, and zucchini. Simmer over low heat for 30 minutes until the meatballs are cooked through.

4 Season the soup with salt and pepper before ladling into bowls.

beef POZOLE

2½ pounds boneless beef shank

5 quarts cold water

1 medium white onion, quartered

½ cup roughly chopped carrot

½ cup roughly chopped celery

3 garlic cloves

2 bay leaves

Salt and freshly ground black pepper

1 (29-ounce can) Mexican-style hominy, drained

2 cups Pasilla-Guajillo Salsa (page 146), or to taste

3 cups thinly sliced green cabbage

1 cup thinly sliced radishes

⅓ cup dried oregano

10 lime wedges

SORRY, MOM, BUT I'M USING CANNED POZOLE (also known as Mexican-style hominy), which makes this incredibly easy to put together. This is traditionally served around Christmastime because it's great for parties and large crowds; serve the shredded beef in the broth and set out all the toppings for people to pick and choose from.

1   Put the beef shank in large heavy pot and add the water, covering completely. Add the onion, carrot, celery, garlic cloves, and bay leaves. Season with 2 tablespoons salt and 1 tablespoon pepper. Bring to a boil, cover, and reduce the heat. Simmer, skimming the fat that comes to the surface while cooking, until the meat is fully cooked and tender, about 2 hours.

2   Remove the meat from the pot and let cool slightly. Strain the broth, discarding the solids, and return to the pot. Add the hominy and bring to a boil.

3   Meanwhile, using a fork, shred the meat into bite-size pieces. Return to the pot along with 1 cup water. Simmer for 5 minutes. Season with salt and pepper. Stir in the salsa.

4   Ladle the pozole into bowls and top with the cabbage, radishes, and oregano. Serve with lime wedges.

shredded brisket IN BROTH

1 pound beef brisket, cut into 3-inch pieces (2¼ cups)

2½ quarts water

2 teaspoons salt

3 garlic cloves, peeled

1 large carrot, cut into ½-inch cubes

2 russet potatoes, quartered

½ cup halved green beans

1 cup fresh corn kernels (from about 1 ear of corn) or thawed frozen

1 cup ½-inch cubed green cabbage

1 medium zucchini, cut into ½-inch cubes

THERE WAS ALWAYS LEFTOVER *CALDO DE RES* in the fridge when I was growing up. My mom would make a huge pot at the beginning of the week and put it in the fridge. My brother, my sister, and I would then help ourselves to a bowl while we watched TV. I used to warm up some tortillas to eat alongside and squeeze some fresh lime juice into the caldo and then sprinkle it with hot sauce.

1 Put the brisket into an 8-quart pot and add the water, salt, and garlic. Bring to a boil, stirring occasionally and skimming the foam from the top. Turn down the heat so that the water simmers and skim again. Simmer over medium-low heat until the meat is cooked through and tender enough to shred, 2½ hours.

2 Using a slotted spoon, transfer the meat to a cutting board. When cool enough to handle, shred the meat.

3 Remove and discard the garlic from the broth. Add enough water to make 4 cups of broth. Bring to a simmer over medium-low heat. Add the carrot, potatoes, and green beans and simmer for 10 minutes. Add the corn, cabbage, and zucchini, and return the meat to the soup. Cook until the vegetables are tender, about 8 minutes.

4 Season with salt and pepper before ladling into bowls.

leftovers?

rolled tacos: Strain the meat from the broth. Stuff the meat into corn tortillas and roll them as you would a cigar. Fry in 350°F vegetable oil until golden brown.

sopa de pasta: In 1 tablespoon vegetable oil, fry some small cooked pasta shape (such as mini elbows) until golden. Add warm beef broth and season with salt and pepper. Add the shredded beef for more protein.

shredded meat salad: Strain the meat from the broth. Toss the meat with olive oil, white vinegar, chopped red onion, chopped serrano chile, cilantro, salt, and pepper. Serve chilled with tostadas.

creamy pinto bean SOUP

serves 4 to 6

I USE CANNED PINTO BEANS but if you have leftover beans made from scratch, feel free to use those. Look for organic canned pinto beans, which are not only better for you but also tend to have better flavor. That drizzle of fresh crema here is absolutely essential at the end. A spoonful of cool crema, warm hearty beans, crunchy tortilla chips, and fresh cilantro equals the perfect bite of classic Mexican comfort food.

2 tablespoons olive oil

1 cup chopped white onion

1 serrano chile

2 garlic cloves, minced

1 (15-ounce) can pinto beans

1 cup vegetable broth

Salt and freshly ground black pepper

½ cup Mexican crema or sour cream

1½ cups tortilla chips

¼ cup fresh cilantro leaves

1 Heat the oil in a large heavy pot over medium-high heat. Add the onion and serrano, and sauté until the onion is tender, about 5 minutes. Add the garlic and cook for 1 minute. Add the beans with the canning liquid and the vegetable broth and bring to a boil. Reduce the heat to medium-low, cover, and simmer until the flavors blend, about 12 minutes. Discard the serrano chile.

2 Transfer to a blender and puree the soup until very smooth. Return the soup to the same pot. Season with salt and pepper.

3 Ladle the soup into bowls. Drizzle with crema and top with tortilla chips and fresh cilantro leaves.

leftovers?

ideo bean soup: Cook some *fideo* (or vermicelli) noodles in the bean soup for a twist on the classic *sopa de fideo*.

cowboy eggs: Fry 2 corn tortillas in vegetable oil until golden brown. Drain excess oil on paper towels. Fry 2 eggs and cook until set. Top each tortilla with a fried egg and pour warm bean sauce on top of each egg. Serve with salsa and crumbled queso fresco or feta.

tortilla SOUP

serves 4 to 6

6 plum tomatoes, cored

1 small white onion, quartered

2 garlic cloves, peeled

Salt and freshly ground pepper

4 cups chicken broth, preferably organic

Vegetable oil, for frying

8 (6-inch) stale corn tortillas (see Note), halved and cut into 2-inch strips

2 Hass avocados, halved, pitted, peeled, and diced

½ cup crumbled queso fresco or feta

½ cup Mexican crema or sour cream

3 dried pasilla chiles, stemmed and cut into 1-inch strips

NOTE Stale tortillas—ones that have been left out overnight—work best for frying. They are less likely to break while frying and get to a nice golden brown color, making for a crunchy tortilla strip. If you don't have time to fry tortillas, just use tortilla chips and crumble them on top of the soup.

WHO DOESN'T LOVE *SOPA DE TORTILLA*? In some recipes, tortillas are actually blended into the soup for extra body and flavor, but I like this lighter version with just the crunchy tortillas on top. For the pasilla chiles you add as a garnish at the end, make sure you give them a couple of minutes to soften in the broth before you bite into them. It's the perfect flavor combo: smoky, slightly bitter chiles, creamy avocado, tart crema, crunchy tortillas, and velvety tomato soup.

1   Bring salted water to a boil in a large saucepan. Add the tomatoes and cook for 5 minutes. Drain the tomatoes and cool slightly. Peel the tomatoes and transfer to a blender. Add the onion, garlic, and 1 teaspoon salt and blend until smooth.

2   Pour the sauce back into the saucepan and add the chicken stock. Bring the soup to a simmer over medium heat. Season with salt and pepper.

3   Pour enough oil into heavy medium skillet to come ½ inch up the sides of the pan. Heat to 350°F. Working in batches, fry the tortilla strips until crisp and golden, about 3 minutes. Using a slotted spoon transfer the strips to paper towels to drain. Sprinkle them with salt while warm.

4   Divide the broth among bowls and serve topped with the tortilla strips, avocado, queso fresco, crema, and pasillas.

roasted cherry tomato
SOUP

serves 4 to 6

4 cups cherry tomatoes

3 tablespoons olive oil

Salt and freshly ground black pepper

½ head of garlic

½ cup chicken or vegetable broth

2 teaspoons chopped fresh thyme

¼ cup Mexican crema or sour cream

1 cup crumbled queso fresco or feta

THE BEST TIME TO MAKE THIS SOUP is in the summer, when cherry tomatoes are at their peak in both flavor and nutrition. You can actually buy a whole bunch of cherry tomatoes, roast them, and freeze them to whip out in the off-season when needed for a variety of dishes. My mom used to make this soup for us all the time, and it wasn't until I started growing thyme in my own home in Tijuana that I added it for even more flavor.

1 Preheat the oven to 400°F.

2 Put the tomatoes on a large rimmed baking sheet. Drizzle with the olive oil and sprinkle generously with salt and pepper. Transfer to the oven. Cut the garlic in half horizontally, put it back together, and wrap in foil. Put the garlic directly on the oven rack alongside the tomatoes. Roast until the tomatoes are golden brown and the garlic is tender, about 45 minutes. Let cool slightly.

3 Transfer the tomatoes and any accumulated juices to a food processor. Squeeze the garlic cloves out of their papery skins into the processor. Pulse until smooth. Transfer the mixture to a heavy medium pot. Add the broth and thyme, and bring to a simmer over medium-high heat. Stir in the crema and season with salt and pepper.

4 Divide the soup among bowls and sprinkle with queso fresco.

leftovers?

cracked eggs in tomato soup: Pour the soup into a skillet and bring to a boil. Crack some eggs into the sauce, then add few slices of queso fresco or feta and some cilantro leaves. Season with salt and pepper. Cover and cook over medium heat until eggs are set. Serve with toast.

whole wheat pasta in tomato-chipotle sauce: Cook some small bacon pieces until crisp. Drain off the fat. Add the soup to the bacon and bring to a boil. Mix in a chopped canned chipotle chile in adobo sauce. Boil until reduced to sauce consistency. Toss with cooked whole-wheat pasta.

spicy shrimp BROTH

serves 6 to 8

BACK IN THE DAY, they used to grind dried whole shrimp in a *molcajete*, a lava mortar and pestle made from volcanic rock; these days, you can find dried shrimp powder in Latin and Asian markets, and even in some supermakets. It's really important to let the shrimp powder cook as long as the recipe calls for, as the flavors intensify and change dramatically from beginning to end.

1 Peel the shrimp, reserving the shells. Put shrimp in a small bowl. Cover and refrigerate.

2 Combine the shrimp shells with the water in a large pot and bring to boil. Reduce the heat and simmer, stirring and the skimming surface occasionally, for 1 hour. Strain the broth into a large bowl, pressing on the solids with the back of a spoon to release as much liquid as possible. Discard the shrimp shells. Return the liquid to the pot.

3 Meanwhile, in a heavy medium skillet, heat the olive oil over medium-high heat. Add the onion and sauté until translucent, 5 minutes. Add the carrot, celery, and bell pepper and sauté until fragrant, 7 minutes. Add the tomato and chiles de árbol and cook for 5 minutes. Mix in the tomato paste and dried shrimp powder and cook for 3 minutes.

4 Stir the sautéed vegetables into the warm shrimp broth in the pot. Cook over medium-low heat for 1½ hours to the concentrate flavors.

5 Add the shrimp to the simmering broth and cook for 3 minutes or until pink and cooked through. Serve in bowls, garnishing with lime wedges.

1 pound jumbo shrimp in the shell, deveined

8 cups water

2 tablespoons olive oil

1 small white onion, chopped

1 medium carrot, peeled and sliced ¼ inch thick

2 celery stalks, diced

1 green bell pepper, seeded and diced

1 medium tomato, cored, seeded, and chopped

4 chiles de árbol, stemmed and chopped

2 tablespoons tomato paste

1 tablespoon dried shrimp powder (see Note)

Lime wedges, for serving

NOTE Shrimp powder is made from ground dehydrated shrimp and is used for seasoning soups, stews, and even cocktails in Mexico—and to flavor noodles and stir-fried dishes in Asia. Don't be put off by its strong, pungent flavor. Once cooked, the flavor mellows into a salty sea flavor that carries a dish.

entrées

i'm obsessed with the scent of

charred poblano peppers. Growing up, I knew that aroma well; it meant we were having Chiles Rellenos (page 98)—roasted poblanos stuffed with gooey melted cheese, battered, and fried—for dinner. I could smell it getting off the school bus and would run all the way home. We often had creamy, crunchy, delicious Roasted Chicken Tostadas (page 81) or Pork Loin in Green Pipian (page 86). And then there were the Mexican-American favorites in our house: Pasilla Bolognese Spaghetti (page 71) made it onto the menu at least once a week. Mexican-style burgers (see page 72) were very much a part of my Tijuana upbringing, too.

In this chapter you'll find a little bit of everything, from the very traditional, such as Stuffed Poblanos in Walnut Sauce (page 75), which is classic Mexican Independence Day fare, to the not-so-much-but-oh-so-delicious Extra Cheesy Mex Mac 'n Cheese (page 101). I've included a recipe for every craving.

pasilla bolognese SPAGHETTI

I'M WELL AWARE THAT WE MEXICANS are not known as pasta-making people, but the truth is that this was one of my all-time-favorite dishes my mom used to make us when we were kids. Pasillas add medium heat and a rich flavor to the meaty bolognese.

serves 6 to 8

1. Heat 2 tablespoons of the olive oil in a heavy medium skillet over medium-high heat. Add the onion and sauté until translucent, about 5 minutes. Add the garlic and cook for 1 minute. Add the tomatoes with their juice, pasillas, and beef broth and cook for 8 minutes for the flavors to incorporate. Transfer to a blender, add the oregano and ½ teaspoon salt, and blend until smooth.

2. Bring a large pot of boiling salted water to a boil.

3. Meanwhile, heat the remaining 2 tablespoons olive oil in the same skillet over medium-high heat and add the meat. Season with salt and pepper. Increase the heat to high and cook, breaking the meat into small pieces with a wooden spoon, until brown, about 12 minutes. Add the pasilla sauce and cook, stirring, for 5 minutes. Stir in the crema and turn off the heat.

4. Cook the pasta in the boiling water according to package instructions until tender but still firm to the bite. Drain, reserving ¼ cup of the pasta water, and return the pasta to the empty pot. Add the pasilla bolognese sauce and the 1 cup Parmesan. Toss over medium heat, adding some of the reserved cooking liquid if the mixture seems dry, until heated through, 8 minutes. Season with salt and pepper.

5. Transfer the pasta to a large shallow serving bowl. Serve, passing additional Parmesan at the table.

4 tablespoons olive oil

2 cups chopped white onion

3 garlic cloves, peeled

1 (28-ounce) can peeled whole tomatoes with juice

5 dried pasilla chiles, stemmed, seeded, and roughly chopped

1½ cups beef broth (preferably organic)

⅛ teaspoon crumbled dried oregano, preferably Mexican

Salt and freshly ground black pepper

1½ pounds ground sirloin

½ cup Mexican crema or sour cream

1 (1-pound) box dried spaghetti

1 cup freshly grated Parmesan cheese, plus more for serving

burgers AL PASTOR

6 dried guajillo chiles, stemmed, seeded, and soaked

2 teaspoons crumbled dried marjoram

2 teaspoons crumbled dried oregano

2 garlic cloves, peeled

1 small white onion, chopped

¾ cup sweetened pineapple juice

Salt and freshly ground black pepper

2 pounds extra-lean ground pork

Vegetable oil

1 pineapple, peeled, cored, and sliced into ½-inch-thick rounds

½ cup mayonnaise

8 sesame seed hamburger buns

1 cup fresh cilantro leaves

WEEKNIGHT DINNERS AT MY HOUSE sometimes involved my mom, dad, brother, sister, and me getting into the car and driving to the corner taqueria. While everybody in my family mostly favored carne asada tacos, I always ordered *tacos al pastor,* or shepherd-style tacos. In a technique similar to cooking gyro meat, pork is very thinly sliced, marinated in a combination of chiles, then stacked and cooked on a vertical rotisserie called a *trompo.* You'll always find pineapple slices at the top of the meat because the drippings not only flavor the pork but also tenderize it. Odds are, like me you don't have a vertical rotisserie at home, so here are all those wonderful flavors in an easy-to-love burger package. Thanks to my friend Chef Spike Mendelsohn for the idea!

1 Drain the chiles and put them in a blender with the marjoram, oregano, garlic, one-fourth of the chopped onion, and the pineapple juice, and puree until smooth. Season the marinade generously with salt and pepper.

2 Put the pork in large bowl and pour the marinade on top. Using a wooden spoon, mix well. Cover with plastic wrap and refrigerate for 30 minutes.

3 Heat a grill pan over medium-high heat.

4 Divide the pork mixture into 8 equal portions. Shape each portion into a ½-inch-thick patty. Oil the grill pan. Working in batches, grill the burgers until cooked through, 6 to 8 minutes per side. Transfer the burgers to a plate and cover with aluminum foil to keep warm. Let rest for about 8 minutes.

5 Meanwhile, brush the grill pan with a little more oil and grill the pineapple slices until golden brown, 2 minutes per side.

6 Spread mayonnaise on the cut sides of each bun and warm on the grill pan for 2 minutes.

7 Top the bottom of each bun with a burger, a slice of grilled pineapple, some cilantro, and some of the remaining chopped onion. Cover with the bun tops and serve.

stuffed poblanos
WITH WALNUT SAUCE

serves 10

THIS DISH WAS BORN IN PUEBLA, at the hands of the nuns of the convent of Santa Monica, in honor of Agustín de Iturbide, our first (and only) emperor. I have a special place in my heart for him because he was born in the city of Valladolid, which is now called Morelia. Considering that the original recipe has close to fifty ingredients, this is certainly an easier version. That said, to get the smooth texture and bright white color of the nogada sauce, you just have to sit for a while and peel those walnuts. Traditionally reserved for Independence Day or other special occasions, probably because of the time-consuming walnut situation, this beautiful dish represents the colors of the Mexican flag.

1   In a heavy large skillet, heat the oil over medium-high heat. Add the onion and sauté until translucent, about 3 minutes. Add the garlic and sauté for 1 minute. Add the pork, beef, bay leaf, and cinnamon stick and season with salt and pepper. Cook over medium heat until the meat loses its pink color and is cooked through, about 7 minutes. Stir in the ground cinnamon, dried apple, apricot, and pineapple and remove from the heat.

2   Boil the walnuts for 1 minute in boiling water and then peel them. Puree the walnuts, crema, and goat cheese in a blender until smooth and silky, about 2 minutes. Season with salt and pepper.

3   Cut a lengthwise slit in each chile and carefully remove the seeds, leaving the stem intact. (For milder heat, cut out the ribs.) Divide the filling among the chiles, then close, overlapping the sides of the openings slightly.

4   Transfer the chiles to plates and pour about ⅓ cup walnut sauce over each. Sprinkle with the parsley and pomegranate seeds. Serve at room temperature.

2 tablespoons vegetable oil

1½ cups chopped white onions

2 garlic cloves, minced

½ pound ground pork

½ pound ground beef

1 bay leaf

1 (3-inch) cinnamon stick

Salt and freshly ground black pepper

1 teaspoon ground cinnamon

⅓ cup chopped dried apple

⅓ cup chopped dried apricots

¾ cup chopped sweetened dried pineapple

4 cups shelled walnuts

2½ cups Mexican crema or sour cream

4 ounces fresh goat cheese, at room temperature

10 poblano chiles, charred and peeled (see Note, page 98)

1 tablespoon chopped fresh parsley

½ cup pomegranate seeds

rib-eye steak WITH
ROASTED GARLIC–ANCHO BUTTER

serves 4

1 head of garlic

16 tablespoons (2 sticks) unsalted butter, at room temperature

2 tablespoons ancho chile powder

Salt and freshly ground black pepper

4 (8- to 10-ounce) rib-eye steaks

2 tablespoons olive oil

IT'S SO EASY TO MAKE A FLAVORED BUTTER, and it makes such a difference in your dishes. Here, roasting the garlic brings out its natural sweetness, making it the ideal paring for smoky, slightly fruity ancho chiles. For more heat and an almost chocolaty flavor, add chipotles; and for more subtle, rich flavors, add a pasilla. You can even add roasted chiles that have been stemmed and seeded, like jalapeños or serranos.

1 Preheat the oven to 400°F.

2 Wrap the head of garlic in aluminum foil and roast in the oven for 40 minutes. Set aside until cool enough to handle.

3 Squeeze the garlic from its papery skins into a medium glass bowl and mix well with the butter and ancho powder. Season with salt and pepper. Put a piece of plastic wrap on a work surface and spoon the butter into the middle. Roll into a cylinder; twist the ends to close, and refrigerate until set, at least 1 hour or up 1 week.

4 Heat 1 tablespoon of the olive oil and 1 tablespoon of the flavored butter in a large heavy skillet over medium-high heat. Sprinkle the steaks generously with salt and pepper. Add 2 steaks and cook for about 6 minutes per side for medium. Transfer to a platter, tent with foil to keep warm, and let rest for 5 minutes. Repeat with remaining 2 steaks.

5 To serve the steaks, top each with a round of the flavored butter.

mexican meatloaf
WITH SALSA GLAZE

serves 6 to 8

2 tablespoons olive oil

½ cup finely chopped white onion

1 medium carrot, finely chopped

1 celery stalk, finely chopped

1 garlic clove, minced

1 pound ground beef

6 ounces raw chorizo, casing removed

2 large eggs, beaten

¾ teaspoon salt

¼ teaspoon freshly ground black pepper

¼ cup ketchup

¼ cup Mexican crema or sour cream

½ cup plain dry bread crumbs

AN ALL-TIME FAVORITE AMERICAN DISH gets a dose of some really Mexican ingredients for what is sure to become one of your weeknight favorites. The addition of the chorizo not only gives the meatloaf a spicy kick, it also keeps it super-moist.

1 Preheat the oven to 375°F.

2 To make the meatloaf, heat the olive oil in heavy medium skillet over medium-high heat. Add the onion, carrot, celery, and chopped garlic. Cook, stirring often, until the vegetables are soft, about 8 minutes. Transfer to a large bowl and let cool slightly. Add the beef and chorizo, and stir to combine.

3 In a medium bowl, combine the eggs, salt, and pepper. Stir in the ketchup and crema. Pour over the meat mixture. Sprinkle the bread crumbs on top and mix thoroughly with clean hands.

4 Pat the mixture into a 9 × 13-inch loaf pan. Bake until an instant-read thermometer inserted into the center of the meatloaf registers 160°F, about 45 minutes. Remove from the oven and carefully pour off any accumulated pan juices.

5 Meanwhile, to make the salsa glaze, heat a heavy medium skillet over high heat. Add the whole tomatoes, onion, garlic cloves, and serrano. Cook, turning frequently, until lightly charred on all sides, about 10 minutes. Remove from the heat. Peel the garlic cloves and transfer to a blender with the charred tomatoes, onion, and serrano. Pulse until chunky, then pour into a small skillet. Stir in the brown sugar, chipotle chile, and mustard. Bring to a boil over medium heat. Cook until slightly thickened, 4 to 5 minutes. Season with salt.

6 Invert the meatloaf onto a cutting board. Slice the meatloaf and arrange on a platter. Spoon the salsa glaze over the top and serve.

SALSA GLAZE

2 medium tomatoes, cored

¼ medium white onion

2 garlic cloves, unpeeled

1 serrano chile, stemmed, seeded, and minced

¼ cup (packed) light brown sugar

1 canned chipotle chile in adobo sauce, minced

1 tablespoon mustard

Salt

leftovers?

meatloaf sandwich: Spread a couple of slices of toast with chipotle mayo. Add a slice of warm meatloaf, some sliced tomatoes, avocado, and iceberg lettuce. Serve with pickled jalapeños.

meatloaf frittata: Whisk 4 eggs and ½ cup crumbled meatloaf, 1 tablespoon chopped fresh cilantro, and ¼ cup grated Monterey Jack cheese. Cook in 1 tablespoon butter in a small skillet over medium heat until just set. Finish under the broiler until golden brown on top.

chiles rellenos de meatloaf: Char, peel, and stem a few Anaheim chiles (see Note, page 98). Stuff each with a good amount of crumbled meatloaf and serve drizzled with Mexican crema and fresh salsa.

ROASTED chicken tostadas

TOSTADAS ARE SIMPLY TORTILLAS that have been cooked until crisp. You can either purchase them already made or take corn tortillas and grill, fry, or bake until nice and crisp. A tostada as a dish—as opposed to the ingredient—is a tostada layered with an array of toppings. This Mexican favorite is my go-to meal when I'm in a rush. I always have shredded roasted organic chicken in the fridge, making this dish a cinch to put together. In terms of toppings, you can add the ones I suggest below, or you can get creative. My mom used to dress her tostadas with a little extra-virgin olive oil and red-wine vinegar. The vinegar gives a nice tangy bite and brightens up the flavors. My sister, Carina, covers her tostadas with heaps of salty Parmesan cheese! I like traditional toppings with tons of fresh avocado and bottled hot sauce.

Spread the tostadas with the refried beans, dividing equally. Top with the chicken, lettuce, onion, radishes, and queso fresco. Drizzle with the crema, top with a dollop of salsa, and serve.

8 tostadas

1 cup refried beans, warmed

4 cups shredded cooked chicken

2 cups shredded iceberg lettuce

1 medium red onion, thinly sliced into rings

8 radishes, thinly sliced

1 cup crumbled queso fresco or feta

½ cup Mexican crema or sour cream

Roasted Apple and Tomatillo Salsa (page 143)

THE 2 A.M. hot dog

4 beef hot dogs

4 slices thick-cut bacon

2 cups finely sliced white onion

4 serrano chiles

Easy Chipotle Mayo (page 141)

4 hot dog buns

1 cup finely chopped tomato

Mustard

Ketchup

THIS IS MEXICAN, I PROMISE. Okay, sort of. It's more like a Mexican tradition that every single teenager has followed after a night of dancing. (I call it the 2 A.M. Hot Dog because my dad might read this and be embarrassed if I call it, more accurately, the 6 A.M. Hot Dog.) There must be a stand selling bacon-wrapped hot dogs outside of every dance spot in Mexico, and those fellas are known to make some serious money in the wee hours of the morning. Ah, the good old times . . .

1 Heat a heavy medium skillet over medium-high heat. Wrap each hot dog with a slice of bacon to enclose the sausage completely. Cook the hot dogs until the bacon is golden brown and cooked through, about 5 minutes per side. Transfer to a plate and wrap tightly with aluminum foil to keep warm.

2 Pour off all but 1 tablespoon of the bacon drippings from the pan. Add the onion, and cook over medium heat, stirring occasionally, until caramelized, about 8 minutes. Add the serranos and cook for 5 more minutes.

3 To assemble each hot dog, spread some mayonnaise on each bun. Put a hot dog in each bun, top with some caramelized onion, a serrano chile, and some fresh tomato. Serve with ketchup and mustard.

BAJA-STYLE braised chicken thighs

serves 4 to 6

CHICKEN THIGHS ARE NOT ONLY INEXPENSIVE but also happen to be really juicy and flavorful. With Baja's Mediterranean climate, capers, olives, and grapes are grown in the beautiful Valle de Guadalupe, and they are now being exported all over the world. Here, you get all those wonderful flavors in an easy-to-prepare dish that's perfect for a weeknight dinner.

1   In a large heavy skillet, heat the olive oil over medium-high heat. Sprinkle the chicken with the oregano and season with salt and pepper.

2   Working in batches, brown the chicken thighs, about 6 minutes per side.

3   Reserve just 2 teaspoons of fat in the pan, discarding any extra. Add the onion and sauté until translucent, 5 minutes. Season with salt and pepper. Add the garlic and cook for 1 minute. Pour in the wine and chicken broth and bring to a boil over medium-high heat, scraping up the browned bits from the bottom of the pan.

4   Return the chicken to the pan. Add the olives and capers. Simmer until the sauce thickens and the chicken is heated through, about 10 minutes.

5   Transfer the chicken to a platter; top with the sauce, and serve.

1 tablespoon olive oil

2 pounds boneless, skinless chicken thighs

1 tablespoon crumbled oregano, preferably Mexican

Salt and freshly ground black pepper

½ medium white onion, finely chopped

3 garlic cloves, minced

1 cup marsala wine

1 cup chicken broth, preferably organic

1 cup mixed olives, pitted

⅓ cup capers, drained

chicken IN EASY ADOBO

serves 4

ADOBO, BY DEFINITION, IS A CHILE PASTE or mixture that you spread on chicken or meat before cooking. Usually it is a mix of chiles, but just using the guajillo makes for easy prep and you still get a wonderful adobo. Flattening the chicken allows you to mark it on the grill (love getting one of those charred pieces of skin!) and also shortens the cooking time. Smear the chicken with the adobo while you cook it and make sure to use all of it up. Serve with warm corn tortillas and slices of queso fresco for some stellar tacos.

1 Preheat the oven to 375°F.

2 Heat the oil in a heavy medium saucepan over medium heat. Add the onion and cook until translucent, about 5 minutes. Add the garlic and cook for 1 minute. Add the chiles and cook until darkened on both sides, about 1 minute.

3 Pour in the broth and bring to a boil. Cook until the chiles are soft, about 5 minutes. Transfer to a blender and puree until smooth. Season with salt and pepper.

4 Heat a large ovenproof grill pan over medium-high heat. Meanwhile, rub half of the adobo mixture all over the chicken. Sear the chicken, breast side down, until grill marks appear, about 6 minutes. Turn the chicken breast side up and transfer to the oven. Roast the chicken, basting with the remaining adobo sauce every 20 minutes, until an instant-read thermometer inserted registers an inner temperature of 180°F, about 40 minutes.

2 tablespoons vegetable oil

1 small white onion, chopped

2 garlic cloves, roughly chopped

10 dried guajillo chiles, stemmed, seeded, and cut into 2-inch pieces

1½ cups chicken broth, preferably organic

Salt and freshly ground black pepper

1 (4-pound) whole chicken, backbone removed, flattened slightly

pork loin IN GREEN PIPIAN

serves 6

1 center-cut boneless pork loin, about 2½ pounds

Salt and freshly ground black pepper

4 garlic cloves

16 slices thick-cut bacon (1-pound package)

1 cup green pumpkin seeds (pepitas)

1 pound tomatillos, husked and rinsed

1 serrano chile, stemmed

½ medium white onion, roughly chopped

1½ cups chicken broth, preferably organic, warmed

1 teaspoon sugar

¼ cup loosely packed fresh cilantro leaves

PIPIAN IS A GREEN SAUCE thickened with pumpkin seeds, kind of like a green mole. It's earthy, thick, and perfect for the fall. Made with tart green tomatillos and fresh cilantro, pipian is a perfect counterpoint for the richness of pork. Once you learn how to make this traditional sauce, you can have fun pairing it with other meats, like grilled chicken or roasted turkey.

1 Preheat the oven to 350°F.

2 Preheat a large heavy ovenproof skillet over medium-high heat. Season the pork loin liberally with salt and pepper. Make 4 slits along the pork loin and insert a garlic clove into each slit. Lay the bacon slices crosswise over the loin, overlapping them slightly and tucking the bacon ends underneath the loin. Sear the pork until bacon starts to color, about 5 minutes per side.

3 Cover roast with aluminum foil and transfer to the oven. Roast until an instant-read thermometer inserted lengthwise into the pork registers 140°F, about 1 hour. Remove from the oven and let rest, covered, for 10 minutes.

4 Meanwhile, heat a large heavy skillet over medium heat. Add the pumpkin seeds and toast, stirring constantly, until they have expanded and begin to pop, 3 to 5 minutes. Transfer to a plate to cool. Set aside 2 tablespoons for garnish.

5 Bring salted water to a boil in a heavy medium saucepan. Add the tomatillos, serrano, and onion and simmer until the tomatillos turn a dark green color, about 10 minutes. Using a slotted spoon, transfer the

ingredients to a blender and puree with the chicken broth, sugar, cilantro, and most of the pumpkin seeds until nearly smooth. Season with salt and pepper.

6 Slice the pork into 2-inch-thick slices and top with the green pipian sauce and the reserved pumpkin seeds.

spiced turkey breast WITH CHOCOLATE PASILLA SAUCE

1 (3½- to 4-pound) bone-in turkey breast half, or 2 bone-in chicken breast halves

4 tablespoons olive oil

1 teaspoon dried oregano

1 teaspoon chili powder

1 teaspoon garlic powder

1 teaspoon onion powder

¼ teaspoon ground cinnamon

Salt and freshly ground black pepper

2½ cups chopped white onions

2 garlic cloves

1 (8-ounce) can tomato sauce

1½ cups chicken broth, preferably organic

5 dried pasilla chiles, soaked

1 (3.1-ounce) disk Mexican chocolate

¼ cup toasted sesame seeds, for garnish

ONE OF MY FAVORITE FLAVOR COMBOS is that of chocolate and chiles, in both sweet and savory dishes. This savory dish is inspired by the traditional flavors of a mole sauce but is made easy. For a special occasion like Thanksgiving or Christmas, make this with turkey. For a great weeknight dinner, substitute chicken. Serve with some Arroz Rojo (page 132) to soak up that extra sauce. This sauce is also wonderful on chicken, so just swap out the turkey breast for the bone-in chicken breasts for another great dinner.

1 Preheat the oven to 375°F.

2 Set a rack in a large roasting pan. Rinse the turkey breast and pat dry. Put the turkey on the rack and drizzle with the 2 tablespoons of the olive oil. In a small bowl, mix the oregano, chili powder, garlic powder, onion powder, cinnamon, ½ teaspoon salt, and ¼ teaspoon pepper. Rub the spice mixture all over the turkey, rubbing some of it underneath the skin.

3 Roast until an instant-read thermometer inserted into thickest part of the turkey registers 165°F and the juices run clear when the turkey is pierced with a fork, 45 to 50 minutes. Remove from the oven and cover tightly with aluminum foil. Let rest for 15 minutes.

4 Meanwhile, heat the remaining 2 tablespoons olive oil in a heavy large saucepan over medium-high heat. Add the onion and sauté for 5 minutes, or until translucent. Add the garlic and cook for 1 minute. Add the tomato sauce and chicken broth and cook over medium-high heat for 8 minutes for the flavors to incorporate. Let cool slightly.

(recipe continues)

5 Drain the pasillas and transfer them to a blender. Add the onion mixture and puree until smooth. Return to same saucepan and add the chocolate, stirring over medium heat until melted. Season with salt and pepper. Remove from the heat.

6 Remove the turkey breast from the bone. Slice into ½-inch-thick slices and transfer to a platter. Top with the chocolate pasilla sauce and sprinkle with sesame seeds and serve.

leftovers?

turkey enchiladas: Stuff warmed tortillas with shredded turkey and top with chocolate pasilla sauce. Drizzle with Mexican crema (or sour cream) and shredded Oaxaca (or mozzarella) cheese and broil.

turkey-rice gratin: Mix shredded turkey with cooked white rice in a baking dish. Top with chocolate pasilla sauce and sprinkle with grated Monterey Jack cheese. Bake at 350°F until heated through, about 30 minutes.

turkey tostadas: Spread some tostadas with warm refried beans. Top with shredded turkey, then drizzle with chocolate pasilla sauce. Top with shredded lettuce, sliced radishes, avocado slices, and diced tomatoes.

cilantro SCALLOPS

THERE'S NOTHING SIMPLER YET MORE ELEGANT than a perfectly cooked scallop. Seared on the outside, sweet and tender on the inside, these scallops shine with just a few ingredients to let the subtle ocean flavor take center stage. When it comes to purchasing scallops, always look for fresh and sustainable choices. When cooking them, it's better to err on the side of slightly undercooking them (I actually prefer them that way), as opposed to overcooking, which makes them incredibly rubbery.

½ cup plus 1 tablespoon olive oil

¼ cup fresh lime juice

1 tablespoon low-sodium soy sauce

½ cup chopped fresh cilantro

1 tablespoon red pepper flakes

4 garlic cloves, minced

1 pound jumbo sea scallops (u/15 count)

Salt and freshly ground black pepper

Lime wedges

1. In a medium bowl, mix ½ cup of the olive oil, the lime juice, soy sauce, cilantro, red pepper flakes, and garlic. Season the scallops with salt and pepper. Add the scallops to the marinade, cover with plastic, and refrigerate for 30 minutes.

2. Heat the remaining 1 tablespoon olive oil in a heavy medium skillet over medium-high heat. Add the scallops and sear until lightly browned and opaque in center, 2 to 3 minutes per side. Discard the marinade. Transfer the scallops to a platter and serve with lime wedges.

GARLICKY BUTTERED baja shrimp

serves 4

KNOWN IN MEXICO AS *CAMARONES AL MOJO DE AJO*, garlic-bathed shrimp are a coastal dish that's a favorite all over the country. I always go to Los Arcos, a restaurant that's been in Tijuana ever since I can remember, to get my fix of this dish, but it is super-easy to pull off at home as well. It makes the whole house smell amazing!

1 Peel the shrimp, keeping the tails intact and reserving the shells.

2 Heat the butter and olive oil in heavy medium skillet over medium heat. Sprinkle the shrimp with salt and pepper. Sauté the shrimp until almost fully cooked, about 3 minutes. Using a slotted spoon, transfer the shrimp to a plate and tent with foil to keep warm.

3 Add the shrimp shells to the skillet and sauté until they turn pink, about 3 minutes. Discard the shells. Add the onion and garlic and sauté until the onion is translucent and the garlic is golden brown, about 6 minutes. Add the wine and bring to a boil, scraping up the browned bits from the bottom of the pan. Boil for 1 minute.

4 Stir in the lime juice and parsley, return the shrimp to the pan, and toss to coat with the sauce. Season with salt and pepper, if necessary.

1 pound medium shrimp (15 to 20 count) in the shell, deveined

2 tablespoons unsalted butter

1 tablespoon olive oil

Salt and freshly ground black pepper

¼ cup minced white onion

8 garlic cloves, minced

3 tablespoons dry white wine

1 tablespoon fresh lime juice

2 tablespoons chopped fresh parsley

leftovers?

hearty burritos: Spread some refried beans on a warm flour tortilla and fill with garlicky shrimp.

linguini with garlicky shrimp: Cook linguini in boiling salted water until al dente. Reheat the shrimp and add to the linguini. Top with chopped fresh cilantro and a drizzle of olive oil.

rice and shrimp salad: Combine the shrimp with cooked white rice, olive oil, and chopped cilantro, scallions, and serrano. Serve at room temperature.

puerto nuevo LOBSTER

16 tablespoons (2 sticks) unsalted butter, cut into pieces

1 cup vegetable oil

6 (10- to 12-ounce) frozen raw lobster tails in the shell, thawed

Garlic salt

Freshly ground black pepper

1 (15.5-ounce) can refried beans, preferably organic, warmed over low heat

Arroz Rojo (page 132)

Salsa Asada (page 148)

MY DAD WORKED HARD DURING THE WEEK, so Sunday was family day. To this day, we often drive down the coast to Puerto Nuevo, a small village just south of Rosarito Beach, known as the lobster capital of Baja. Lobster is brought in from the ocean that morning, cleaned, cooked in lard, and served with rice, beans, clarified butter, and some warm homemade flour tortillas. It's a festive spot: *Trios* are always in the background, signing boleros, ballads, and rancheras to the locals and tourists alike, and every table sports plenty of micheladas and margaritas.

1 To make clarified butter, put half of the butter in a 4-cup glass measuring cup. Microwave on high for 2 minutes. Remove from the microwave and let stand for 1 minute. Spoon off the foamy top layer and discard. Spoon the clear (clarified) butter into a small bowl. Discard any milky liquid at the bottom of the measuring cup.

2 Heat the oil in a large heavy skillet over medium-high heat. Add the remaining butter and melt until foamy. Season the lobster tails heavily with garlic salt and pepper. Working in two batches, fry each lobster tail, meat side down, until golden about, 5 minutes. Turn over onto the shell side and fry until the meat is opaque, 3 minutes. Transfer to paper towels to drain.

3 Serve the lobster tails with refried beans, Arroz Rojo, and the salsa. Pass the clarified butter to drizzle over the lobster.

sweet ancho chiles
IN BLACK BEAN SALSA

USUALLY, STUFFED CHILE RECIPES call for roasted fresh chiles, but I also love hydrating dried ones and using those. Brown sugar not only mellows the spice in the anchos, it also makes for a great paring with the fresh cheese and the hearty bean sauce. My grandfather always used to make these for Christmas.

1 Mix the brown sugar and 3 cups hot water in an 8-inch glass baking dish, stirring until the sugar is completely dissolved. Cut a lengthwise slit in each chile and carefully remove the seeds, leaving the stem intact. (For milder heat, carefully cut out the ribs.) Add the anchos to the baking dish. Using an ovenproof pot, weight the chiles down so they absorb as much liquid as possible. Let stand for 2 hours.

2 Meanwhile, heat the oil in a heavy medium skillet over medium-high heat. Add the onion and sauté until translucent, 5 minutes. Add the garlic and cook for 1 minute. Add the tomatoes and cook for 5 minutes for the flavors to incorporate. Lower the heat to medium, mix in the beans, marjoram, and broth, and simmer for 8 minutes. Turn off the heat and let cool for 5 minutes.

3 Transfer the bean mixture to a blender and process until smooth. Season with salt and peeper. Return to same pan and keep warm until serving.

4 Drain the anchos and pat dry; discard the liquid. Spoon some bean salsa on a platter and carefully arrange the chiles over the salsa. Carefully fill each chile with about ⅓ cup cheese. Enclose as tightly as possible. Serve warm or at room temperature.

½ cup (packed) dark brown sugar

6 dried ancho chiles

2 tablespoons vegetable oil

1 small white onion, quartered

2 garlic cloves, minced

2 plum tomatoes, cored and roughly chopped

1 (15.5-ounce) can black beans, preferably organic

¼ teaspoon dried marjoram

¼ cup chicken broth, preferably organic

Salt and freshly ground black pepper

12 ounces queso fresco or feta, cubed

chiles RELLENOS

serves 6

6 poblano chiles, charred and peeled (see Note)

8 ounces Monterey Jack cheese

½ cup all-purpose flour

Salt and freshly ground black pepper

Vegetable oil

4 large egg whites

4 large egg yolks, beaten

1 (15.5-ounce) can peeled tomatoes, drained

1 small white onion, cut into 8 wedges

2 garlic cloves, peeled

3 cups chicken broth, preferably organic

NOTE To char poblano chiles (or any other fresh chiles), simply place them over a gas flame or underneath the broiler and cook until they are blackened on all sides. Enclose them in a plastic bag and let stand for 10 minutes (this will steam the peppers and make them easier to peel).

MY MOTHER OFTEN MADE THIS signature Mexican dish during the week, with either cheese or ground meat. The key here is beating the egg whites to stiff peaks to get that fluffy coating. The addition of the yolk is a trick I use to get more of a golden color.

1 Carefully cut a lengthwise slit in each poblano and scoop out the seeds. Cut the Monterey Jack into 2-inch-long sticks that are about 1 inch wide. Stuff each poblano with 2 to 3 sticks of cheese, depending on the size of the chile, enclosing it tightly.

2 Put the flour on a plate and season with salt and pepper. Dredge the chiles in the flour.

3 Pour 2 inches of oil into a 12-inch heavy skillet and heat over medium-low heat to 375°F.

3 Meanwhile, using a hand-held mixer, beat the egg whites to soft peaks. Beat the yolks into the whites along with ¼ teaspoon salt. Beat for 3 minutes on high speed until they hold stiff peaks. Holding each poblano by the stem, dip it into the egg mixture to coat completely.

4 Fry the poblanos, turning once, until golden brown all over, about 2 minutes per side. Use a slotted spoon to transfer to paper towels to drain.

5 Combine the tomatoes, onion, garlic, chicken broth, and 1 teaspoon salt in a blender and puree until smooth. Transfer to a medium saucepan and bring to a boil over medium-high heat. Boil until slightly reduced, about 5 minutes. Season with salt and pepper.

6 Divide the poblanos among 6 plates. Spoon the sauce over the chiles and serve.

extra-cheesy MEX MAC 'N CHEESE

I LOVE HOMEMADE MAC 'N CHEESE, AS DOES MY SON. With three different kinds of cheeses and a chile-thyme bread-crumb topping, this version is popular with adults and kids alike.

1 Heat 4 tablespoons of the butter in a medium skillet over medium-high heat. Add the shallots and sauté until translucent, 5 minutes. Mix in the bread crumbs to coat with the butter, add the ancho powder and fresh thyme, and season with salt. Set aside.

2 Preheat the oven to 350°F. Grease a 9 × 13-inch glass baking dish with 1 tablespoon of the butter.

3 Bring a large pot of salted water to a boil. Add the macaroni and cook according to package instructions until tender but still firm to the bite. Drain well.

4 Meanwhile, melt the remaining 4 tablespoons butter in a large heavy pot over medium-high heat. Add the flour and stir for 1 minute; do not brown. Whisk in the milk in a slow steady stream. Bring to a simmer, then reduce the heat to low, and cook, whisking often, until the sauce thickens, about 10 minutes. Whisk in 1 cup of the mozzarella, 1 cup of the Cheddar, and 1 cup of the Manchego. Season generously with salt and pepper. Stir in the pasta and pour into the prepared baking dish.

5 Mix the remaining 1 cup mozzarella, 1 cup Cheddar, and 1 cup Manchego in a medium bowl. Sprinkle over the pasta. Top with the bread crumbs. Cover with foil and bake for 30 minutes. Uncover and bake until the top is golden, 12 minutes. Serve immediately.

9 tablespoons unsalted butter

3 large shallots, minced

1½ cups plain dry bread crumbs

2 tablespoons ancho powder

2 teaspoons chopped fresh thyme

Salt and freshly ground black pepper

1 (1-pound) package mini elbow macaroni

¼ cup all-purpose flour

1 quart whole milk

2 cups shredded mozzarella cheese

2 cups shredded Cheddar cheese

2 cups shredded mild Manchego cheese

corn and poblano
LASAGNE

3 tablespoons unsalted butter

3 garlic cloves, minced

2 cups fresh corn kernels (from about 2 ears) or thawed frozen

1½ cups heavy cream

1 teaspoon chopped fresh thyme

Salt and freshly ground black pepper

½ cup thinly sliced white onion

1 large zucchini, thinly sliced lengthwise

3 poblano chiles, charred and peeled (see Note, page 98), stemmed, seeded, and cut into 1-inch strips

12 (7 × 3-inch) no-boil lasagna noodles

2 cups shredded Oaxaca cheese or mozzarella

THIS RECIPE COMES FROM MY TRUSTED RIGHT-HAND GAL, Valeria "Vale" Linss. She heads my culinary team, coming up with these wonderful ideas to try—and this Mexican lasagne has to be one of my favorites. Vale studied at some fancy Italian cooking school, where she made pasta from scratch every day and mastered the perfect gnocchi. And yet for this easy recipe, she agrees that no-boil lasagna noodles are the way to go.

1 Preheat the oven to 350°F.

2 Melt 1 tablespoon of the butter in a heavy medium saucepan over medium heat. Add two-thirds of the garlic and sauté for 1 minute. Mix in the corn and sauté for 5 minutes. Stir in the cream and thyme. Cook over medium-low heat for 5 minutes for the flavors to incorporate. Turn off the heat and let cool slightly. Transfer to a blender and puree until smooth. Season with salt and pepper.

3 Heat the remaining 2 tablespoons butter in a small heavy skillet over medium heat. Add the onion and sauté until translucent, 5 minutes. Add the remaining garlic and cook for 1 minute. Mix in the zucchini and poblano strips, and cook for 5 minutes to blend the flavors. Season with salt and pepper.

4 Spread about one-fourth of the corn mixture over the bottom of an 11 × 8-inch baking dish. Cover with a layer of 3 lasagna sheets. Spread one-fourth of the poblano mixture and one-fourth of the cheese over the pasta. Repeat the layering three more times. Bake until browned and the pasta is cooked, 50 minutes. Let stand for 15 minutes before serving.

chipotle-plum bbq ribs
WITH BRUSSELS SPROUT SLAW

serves 2

RIBS

¼ **cup hot water**

1 **teaspoon instant coffee**

¾ **cup plum sauce (see Note)**

½ **cup fresh orange juice**

2 **tablespoons adobo sauce (from canned chipotle chiles)**

1 **tablespoon brown sugar**

Salt and freshly ground black pepper

2½ **pounds baby back ribs**

NOTE Plum sauce, which has a sweet-tart flavor, can be found in well-stocked supermarkets in the Asian foods aisle.

EVERY CULTURE HAS IT OWN TWIST ON BARBECUE, the slow cooking of meat on some type of rustic grill for long periods of time that results in such a tasty and tender piece of smoked meat. In Mexico we have the traditional *barbacoa*, slow-cooked goat served with a tomato-based sauce, tortillas, lime wedges, and pickled veggies. In this recipe, I combine my Mexican and American heritages to make some sweet and spicy, cooked-to-perfection ribs that have become one of my dad's favorite dishes. Admittedly, it's not true slow-and-low barbecue, but you still get a ton of flavor in the oven. These ribs pair nicely with the Yukon Potato, Poblano, and Corn Gratin (page 128).

1 Preheat the oven to 350°F.

2 To prepare the ribs, mix the hot water with the instant coffee in a small saucepan, and stir to dissolve the coffee. Mix in the plum sauce, orange juice, adobo sauce, and brown sugar and then bring to a boil over medium heat. Reduce the heat and simmer for 5 minutes until slightly thickened. Season to taste with salt and pepper.

3 Coat both sides of the ribs with the sauce, saving ⅔ cup for basting. Arrange the ribs, meaty side up, in one layer on a foil-lined baking sheet. Cover the ribs tightly with foil and bake for 1 hour. Remove the foil from the top, baste the ribs with the remaining sauce, and bake the ribs for another hour until very tender.

4 Meanwhile, to make the slaw, stem and seed the ancho chiles. Use kitchen shears to snip them into rings. Toss with the Brussels sprouts and olive oil, season with salt and pepper, and spread out in a single layer on a baking sheet. Roast alongside the ribs in the oven for 15 minutes, until tender and golden brown. Remove from the oven and let cool for 10 minutes.

5 Combine the sour cream, mayonnaise, vinegar, and honey in a medium bowl. Season the dressing with salt and pepper. Toss the Brussels sprouts and chiles with dressing until well combined. Refrigerate to chill while the ribs finish cooking.

6 Remove the ribs from the over and allow them to rest for 10 to 15 minutes. Cut between the ribs and serve with the Brussels sprout slaw.

SLAW

3 ancho chiles

1 pound Brussels sprouts, thinly sliced

¼ cup olive oil

Salt and freshly ground black pepper

2 tablespoons sour cream

2 tablespoons mayonnaise

1 teaspoon apple cider vinegar

2 teaspoons honey

sides and
salads

honestly, we Mexicans are not a salad people. And yet, ironically, the one salad everyone knows and loves almost the world over—Caesar salad, that is—is Mexican! Victor's Caesar Salad (page 111) is my replica of the dish I used to have many Sundays with my family at the one and only Victor's Restaurant when I was a kid. You'll find recipes both light and hearty in this chapter and a beautiful Roasted Butternut Squash Salad with Tangerine-Rosemary Vinaigrette (page 114) that just shouldn't be missed.

The sides, like the wildly colorful Corn and Zucchini Sauté (page 120), can complement any menu, not just a Mexican one, which is something I could easily say about most of the recipes in this book. Just start with fresh ingredients, preferably in season and local, add a simply grilled piece of fish, chicken, or meat, and you've got a memorable dinner in no time.

red and white kidney bean SALAD

serves 4 to 6

I LOVE HEARTY BEAN SALADS, which are mostly seen in the northern parts of Mexico, because you can add virtually anything you want to them. I always have organic canned beans on hand and will mix in whatever I have in the pantry or whatever fresh herbs are growing in my backyard. You can use this very simple salad almost like a base, adding grilled chicken, canned tuna, seared steaks, or grilled shrimp to make a main dish.

½ cup finely chopped red onion

¼ cup chopped fresh cilantro

2 serrano chiles, stemmed, seeded, and finely chopped

2 garlic cloves, minced

2 tablespoons fresh lime juice

1 tablespoon red wine vinegar

¼ cup olive oil

1 (15-ounce) can white kidney beans, rinsed and drained

1 (15-ounce) can red kidney beans, rinsed and drained

Salt and freshly ground black pepper

In a medium glass bowl, whisk together the onion, cilantro, serranos, garlic, lime juice, vinegar, and olive oil. Add the beans and stir to combine. Season with salt and pepper. Serve at room temperature.

victor's caesar SALAD

serves 4

WHEN I WAS A KID GROWING UP IN TIJUANA, there was one place you went when you wanted the best Caesar salad around: Victor's restaurant. Although they did not create the dish (that happened many years before, at another Tijuana restaurant owned by Caesar Cardini), Victor's sure had the version that my family and almost everyone else I knew favored. Baja chef and close friend Javier Plascencia rescued the recipe and shared it with me to cook on my show. He's now serving Victor's original version at his Tijuana restaurant, Caesar's Restaurant Bar.

2 large eggs

2 tablespoons mayonnaise

2 teaspoons Worcestershire sauce

1 teaspoon steak sauce

1 teaspoon bottled hot sauce

1 teaspoon red wine vinegar

½ cup corn oil

Salt and freshly ground black pepper

4 romaine lettuce hearts, leaves separated

¼ cup grated cotija or Parmesan cheese

1 Bring a small saucepan of water to a boil over medium-high heat. Add the eggs and boil for 5 minutes. Remove the eggs form the water and set aside until cool enough to handle, about 7 minutes.

2 Peel the eggs and cut in half. Spoon the yolks, which will still be slightly soft, into a blender; reserve the whites for another use. Add the mayonnaise, Worcestershire sauce, steak sauce, hot sauce, and vinegar. Pulse until blended. With the machine running, drizzle in the oil and process until smooth. Season with salt and pepper.

3 Put the lettuce and cheese in a large salad bowl. Add the dressing and gently toss to coat. Serve immediately.

steak and wilted spinach salad WITH SERRANO-MINT DRESSING

serves 4

4 (6-ounce) boneless sirloin steaks

Salt and freshly ground black pepper

Serrano-Mint Dressing (recipe follows)

1 tablespoon olive oil

6 strips bacon, diced

2 shallots, thinly sliced

12 cups loosely packed spinach

GRILLED, MARINATED SIRLOIN STEAKS, tossed in a delicious serrano, honey, and mint dressing and mixed with healthy spinach, salty bacon, and lightly grilled shallots, make for a main-course salad with lots of punch.

1 Sprinkle the steaks liberally with salt and pepper. Put them in a glass baking dish and spread all over with 3 tablespoons of the dressing. Let stand at room temperature for 1 hour or cover and place in the refrigerator overnight.

2 Heat the olive oil in a heavy medium skillet over medium-high heat. Working in two batches, cook the steaks to desired doneness, about 7 minutes per side for medium. Transfer to a cutting board and let rest for 5 minutes. Cut into ¾-inch-thick slices.

3 Meanwhile, wipe out the skillet. Add the bacon and cook until crisp, about 7 minutes. Transfer to a paper-lined plate. Drain excess fat from the pan, add the shallots, and sauté until golden, about 10 minutes. Turn off the heat, add the spinach, and turn frequently until wilted.

4 Transfer the spinach and shallots to a platter, sprinkle with the bacon bits, and top with the sliced steak. Drizzle some of the remaining vinaigrette on top and serve immediately.

serrano-mint dressing

THE COMBINATION OF FRESH MINT AND CILANTRO, spicy serrano, sweet honey, and tangy soy sauce and vinegar creates a flavorful dressing that is delicious on any grilled meat. Serrano peppers are hotter than jalapeños, ranging from hot to very hot, so adjust the amount you use to suit your taste.

Combine the mint, cilantro, serrano, honey, soy sauce, and vinegar in a blender and process until smooth. With the blender running, add the olive oil and mix until emulsified, about 1 minute.

1⅓ cups loosely packed fresh mint leaves

⅔ cup loosely packed fresh cilantro leaves

½ to 1 serrano pepper, to taste, stemmed and seeded

4 teaspoons honey

1 tablespoon low-sodium soy sauce

2 teaspoons distilled white vinegar

½ cup olive oil

roasted butternut squash
salad WITH TANGERINE-ROSEMARY VINAIGRETTE

serves 4

1½ pounds butternut squash, peeled, seeded, and cut into 1-inch cubes (about 4 cups)

4 tablespoons olive oil

3 tablespoons roughly chopped fresh rosemary

Salt and freshly ground black pepper

4 tangerines

6 cups fresh spinach, loosely packed

¼ cup dried cranberries

THIS HEARTY AUTUMN/WINTER SALAD bursts with bright flavors thanks to juicy tangerines, tart cranberries, and piney rosemary. Most of the butternut squash we ate at my house growing up came from the markets in San Diego, as we don't have butternut squash in northern Mexico. It is available in southern Mexico, however, where it's known as *calabaza vinatera,* as it was often hollowed out, dried, and used to store wine.

1 Preheat the oven to 400°F.

2 Toss the squash with 2 tablespoons of the olive oil on a baking sheet and spread in an even layer. Season with 2 tablespoons of the rosemary and salt and pepper. Roast, stirring once halfway, until the squash is just tender and golden, about 20 minutes. Remove from the oven and cool until warm, about 15 minutes.

3 While the squash is roasting, peel 3 of the tangerines and slice them crosswise into ½-inch-thick rounds, removing any seeds. Juice the remaining tangerine and whisk together with the remaining 2 tablespoons olive oil and remaining 1 tablespoon rosemary. Season with salt and pepper.

4 Combine the warm squash, the spinach, tangerine slices, and cranberries with the dressing and toss gently to coat. Divide among salad plates.

roasted cauliflower WITH
AVOCADO-CILANTRO DIP

I LOVE HOW ROASTING VEGETABLES brings out their natural sweetness and eliminates any bitterness. Try this dip with any of your favorite vegetables. In addition to cauliflower, I especially love Brussels sprouts, broccoli, and cabbage. Incredibly healthy and super easy, this makes for a perfect after-school snack.

1 Preheat the oven to 400°F.

2 Put the cauliflower, oil, and oregano in a large bowl. Sprinkle with salt and pepper and toss to combine. Spread in a single layer on large baking sheet and roast, turning occasionally, until tender and golden brown, about 30 minutes. Let cool and then transfer to platter.

3 Meanwhile, in the bowl of a food processor, combine the avocado, cream cheese, serrano, cilantro, and lime juice and blend until smooth and creamy. Season with salt and pepper. Transfer to a small bowl and serve with the cauliflower for dipping.

1 (2-pound) head cauliflower, cut into 1½-inch florets

3 tablespoons olive oil

1 teaspoon dried oregano, preferably Mexican

Salt and freshly ground black pepper

1 Hass avocado, halved, pitted, and peeled

4 ounces cream cheese, at room temperature

1 serrano chile, stemmed and seeded

½ cup chopped fresh cilantro

1 tablespoon fresh lime juice

leftovers?

cauliflower cream soup: Heat cauliflower and some vegetable broth in a saucepan, then puree in a blender and season with salt and pepper. Top with a dollop of the avocado-cilantro dip.

cauliflower gratin: Mix cauliflower with a little cream, shredded mozzarella cheese, and plain bread crumbs in a buttered glass baking dish. Bake at 375°F until the cheese is golden brown.

cauliflower mash: Combine cauliflower with milk, a little water, and a pat of butter in a saucepan. Bring to a boil and cook until very soft. Puree until smooth. Season with salt and pepper.

CREAMY mexican corn

serves 2

2 ears of corn

2½ teaspoons fresh lime juice

2 tablespoons Mexican crema or sour cream

2 tablespoons mayonnaise

4 tablespoons (½ stick) unsalted butter, at room temperature

Salt and freshly ground black pepper

½ cup crumbled queso fresco or feta

Chili-lime powder (optional), for serving

ONE OF THE MANY THINGS I MISS about my mom is her wacky, spur-of-the-moment food cravings. My brother, sister, and I would be at home watching TV or doing our homework and she'd have a craving for *esquites*. She'd pack us up in the car and off we'd go in search of a street cart with creamy corn cups. Traditionally, the corn is boiled in huge pots and you can smell it a block away. But lately, you can find *esquites asados,* or grilled creamy corn, at many of the stands. I prefer them grilled and always ask for extra butter and mayo.

1 Preheat a griddle over moderately high heat. Roast the corn on the dry griddle until slightly blackened in spots, about 5 minutes per side. Let cool slightly.

2 Cut the kernels off the cobs. Mix the lime juice, crema, mayonnaise, and butter in a large bowl until combined. Add the warm corn kernels, season with salt and pepper, and toss to combine.

3 Divide corn between 2 cups. Top each with queso fresco, dividing equally. Sprinkle with chile-lime powder and serve.

corn and zucchini SAUTÉ

serves 4 to 6

2 strips of bacon, chopped

½ cup finely minced white onion

1 garlic clove, minced

2 medium tomatoes, cored, seeded, and chopped

2 cups fresh corn kernels (from about 2 ears)

4 small zucchini, sliced into ¼-inch-thick rounds

2 tablespoons chopped fresh cilantro

Salt and freshly ground black pepper

A VERSION OF THIS VEGETABLE-PACKED SIDE DISH is found in every house across Mexico. Although Fausto is not a picky eater, the addition of crispy, savory bacon to this dish has made it one of his absolute favorite sides. I use Mexican calabazas, which can be substituted for regular zucchini.

1 Preheat a heavy medium sauté pan over medium heat. Add the bacon and cook, stirring to render the fat, until crisp, about 5 minutes. Using a slotted spoon, transfer the bacon to a paper towel–lined plate to drain. Remove all but 2 tablespoons of bacon drippings from the pan.

2 Sauté the onion in the bacon drippings over medium-high heat until translucent, 5 minutes. Add the garlic and cook for 1 minute. Add the tomatoes, corn, and zucchini and cook, stirring occasionally, until the zucchini is tender, about 5 minutes.

3 Stir in the cilantro and season with salt and pepper. Mix in the bacon and serve.

leftovers?

zucchini, corn, and bacon frittata: Mix vegetables with 4 beaten eggs and 2 tablespoons Mexican crema or sour cream. Pour the mixture into a preheated nonstick medium skillet and cook, lifting the edges with a spatula, until the frittata is partly cooked, about 8 minutes. Transfer the pan to a 400°F oven and bake until puffed and golden, 8 to 10 minutes.

zucchini, corn, and cilantro penne: Mix vegetables with cooked penne and top with shaved Parmesan cheese.

zucchini and corn quesadillas: Mix vegetables with Monterey Jack cheese and stuff between flour tortillas before heating on the stove-top in a large skillet until the cheese melts.

creamed zucchini and corn: Add 2 tablespoons Mexican crema or sour cream to the corn and zucchini. Use as a topping for grilled chicken breasts.

rice and zucchini casserole: Mix vegetables with cooked white rice and bake with shredded Monterey Jack cheese at 375°F until cheese melts, about 20 minutes.

acorn squash and roasted garlic MASH

2 acorn squash, halved crosswise and seeded

1 head of garlic

7 tablespoons unsalted butter

2 teaspoons chopped fresh thyme

Salt and freshly ground black pepper

1 leek. white and pale green parts only, diced

1 Gala apple, cut into ½-inch pieces

ACORN SQUASH IS COMMON IN SOUTHERN MEXICO. I like to puree it with roasted garlic and thyme and garnish it with a sauté of crisp Gala apples and leeks. Actually, similar flavors often show up in *crema de calabaza,* a Spanish squash soup, served in the cold winter months, that I tried the first time I went to Valladolid (my last name is actually a city).

1 Preheat the oven to 400°F.

2 Put the acorn squash halves, cut side down, on rimmed baking sheets and transfer to the oven. Pour a little water into the baking sheets to coat the bottoms; this will help steam the squash so they don't dry out and will be easy to mash. Wrap the garlic in foil and place directly on the rack next to the squash. Roast both the squash and garlic until very tender, about 1 hour. Let both cool slightly.

3 Scoop the squash flesh into a large bowl. Unwrap the garlic and squeeze the cloves from the papery skins into the bowl. Add 6 tablespoons of the butter and mash until smooth. Stir in the thyme and season with salt and pepper. Spoon into a serving bowl and keep warm.

4 Melt the remaining 1 tablespoon butter in a small heavy skillet over medium-high heat. Add the leek and apple, and sauté until crisp tender, 6 minutes. Season with salt and pepper. Top the puree with the apple pieces and serve.

potato-achiote CROQUETTES

serves 4 to 6

MY MOM PICKED UP THIS RECIPE—originally a dish from Ecuador—in her travels to South America. While she had it served with chorizo and a sunny-side up egg on top, I like this healthier version, which is topped with crisp and peppery arugula and drizzled with olive oil and fresh lime juice to brighten it up. Serve this as a side with a warm soup for a balanced lunch.

1½ pounds Yukon Gold potatoes

Salt and freshly ground black pepper

¼ cup plus 3 tablespoons olive oil

⅓ cup finely minced white onion

1 garlic clove, minced

2 teaspoons achiote paste (see Note)

4 ounces mozzarella cheese, shredded (1 cup)

2 cups arugula

2 limes, halved

1 Put the potatoes in a heavy medium pot and cover with cold water. Season the water with salt and bring to a boil over high heat. Reduce the heat to medium and simmer the potatoes until very tender, about 30 minutes.

2 Meanwhile, heat 2 tablespoons of the olive oil in large heavy skillet over medium heat. Add the onion and cook until softened, about 5 minutes. Add the garlic and cook for 1 minute. Mix in the achiote paste and remove from the heat.

3 Drain the potatoes and then peel them. Mash in a large bowl with a fork or potato masher. Add the onion mixture and mozzarella and stir to combine. To form the croquettes, divide the mixture into 8 balls and flatten each into 3-inch patties.

4 Heat 1 tablespoon of the olive oil in a 12-inch skillet over medium-high heat until hot. Working in two batches, pan-fry the croquettes, turning once, until a crust forms, about 3 minutes per side. Transfer to paper towels to drain.

5 Carefully transfer the hot croquettes to plates. Top with arugula, dividing equally. Drizzle with the remaining ¼ cup olive oil, squeeze lime juice over each, and sprinkle with salt and pepper before serving.

NOTE Achiote paste comes from ground achiote seeds, also known as annatto seeds. Available in East Indian markets, Latin markets, and some supermarkets, achiote paste not only adds musky, earthy flavor to a dish, it also adds a brick-red color. In Mexico, it is often used by cooks in Yucatán, where it is mixed with the bright, citrus juice of bitter oranges or limes and then used to spread on fish for grilling or pork for roasting.

chayote WITH YOGURT DIP

serves 4 to 6

1 pound chayote (about 4 medium), each cut lengthwise into 6 wedges

1 cup roughly chopped green bell pepper

½ avocado, pitted and peeled

½ teaspoon ground cumin

¾ cup plain yogurt

¼ cup mayonnaise

Salt and freshly ground black pepper

GROWN IN CALIFORNIA, chayote—also known as pear squash, Mexican squash, or even vegetable pear—are now found in many supermarkets across the country. Chayote can be eaten raw in salads but I prefer them steamed or boiled. They are mild, so feel free to add extra cumin to the dip if you want more assertive flavors.

1 Bring a medium pot of salted water to a boil. Add the chayote wedges and boil until tender when pierced with a sharp knife, about 10 minutes. Strain and set aside to cool slightly, about 8 minutes.

2 Combine the bell pepper, avocado, cumin, yogurt, and mayonnaise in a food processor and blend until smooth. Season with salt and pepper. Transfer to a serving bowl and let stand for 10 minutes to thicken.

3 Serve the chayote with the yogurt sauce for dipping.

leftovers?

fried chayote: Coat cooked chayotes in flour, then in beaten egg, and finally in plain bread crumbs. Pan fry in 350°F vegetable oil until golden brown. Serve warm or at room temperature with the yogurt dip or plain mayo.

healthy chayote salad: Combine with hearts of palm and roasted bell peppers. Toss with olive oil, a splash of red wine vinegar, and some crumbled dried oregano, preferably Mexican.

chayote pico de gallo: Mix with chopped red onion, cilantro, chopped serrano chile, fresh lime juice, and olive oil. Use as a topping for grilled chicken.

roasted baby red potatoes
WITH CHIPOTLE BUTTER

I LOVE POTATOES but usually don't have the time or the patience to peel them. That's why I often opt for baby potatoes so I can just leave the skin on. Their thin, undeveloped skins not only add another layer of texture and flavor, they also add color. The chipotle cilantro butter here is smoky, spicy, and delicious. I always make a little extra for smearing on grilled corn or bread.

4 tablespoons (½ stick) unsalted butter, at room temperature

½ teaspoon chipotle powder

1 teaspoon chopped fresh cilantro

Salt and freshly ground black pepper

2 pounds baby red potatoes

½ cup olive oil

1 Mix the butter, chipotle powder, cilantro, and ¼ teaspoon salt in a small bowl. Put a square piece of plastic wrap on a work surface. Spoon the chipotle butter over the plastic and roll into a 1-inch-thick diameter log. Refrigerate until firm, about 2 hours.

2 Preheat the oven to 450°F.

3 Cut the potatoes in half and toss them with olive oil; season with salt and pepper. Roast on a baking sheet until tender and cooked through, 30 minutes.

4 Transfer the potatoes to a platter. Cut the chipotle butter into pieces, toss with the hot potatoes until melted, and serve.

leftovers?

chipotle mashed potatoes: Combine the potatoes and chipotle butter with a little bit of warm milk and mash until nice and smooth. Season with salt and pepper.

potato omelet: Slice the cooked potatoes into 1-inch rounds and fry them in chipotle butter until golden brown. Add beaten eggs and some Manchego cheese. Cook for 5 minutes over medium-low heat, then flip and cook for 5 minutes longer.

potato and chorizo quesadillas: Sauté leftover potatoes with some sliced chorizo in the chipotle butter and use as a filling for quesadillas.

yukon potato, poblano, and corn GRATIN

3 teaspoons olive oil

1 cup fresh corn kernels
(from about 1 ear)

3 large poblano chiles,
charred, stemmed, seeded,
and cut into strips (see
page 98)

Salt and freshly ground black
pepper

4 Yukon Gold potatoes
(about 1 pound), peeled and
sliced ⅛ inch thick

3 cups coarsely grated
Oaxaca cheese or whole-milk
mozzarella

½ cup half-and-half

½ cup Mexican crema or
sour cream

I COULD SIT DOWN WITH THIS GRATIN and eat the whole thing. It's rich, creamy, spicy, and smoky and a superb accompaniment for Thanksgiving turkey. The beauty of the gratin is that you can assemble and cook the whole thing the day ahead, then reheat it at 350°F for thirty minutes before serving.

1 Preheat the oven to 400°F. Coat a 9½-inch round deep-dish glass pie dish or cast-iron skillet with 2 teaspoons of the oil.

2 Heat the remaining 1 teaspoon oil in a large nonstick skillet over medium-high heat. Add the corn and sauté until tender, 5 minutes. Add the poblano strips and season with salt and pepper. Remove from the heat.

3 Arrange one-third of the potato slices, overlapping slightly, in the prepared dish. Sprinkle half of poblano mixture over, and top with one-third of the cheese. Repeat, adding a second layer of potatoes, the rest of the poblano mixture, and a second layer of cheese. Stir together the half-and-half and crema and season with salt and pepper. Pour into the dish and top with the remaining cheese.

4 Put the pie dish on a rimmed baking sheet and cover the dish tightly with foil. Bake 30 for minutes. Remove the foil and continue baking until the potatoes are tender and the cheese is golden brown, about 25 minutes. Let stand for 10 minutes before serving.

crimini mushrooms
STUFFED WITH CHARD

serves 4 to 6

I LOVE TO COOK CHARD, known in Mexico as *acelgas,* with garlic and bacon, then mix it with requesón, our version of ricotta cheese. These flavorful little bites would make for a perfect appetizer for your Thanksgiving menu or when having a cocktail party with friends. Feel free to substitute a little bit of cooked chorizo for the bacon; it would add even more Mexican flavor and is also a great balance to the creamy, lightly sweet flavor of the requesón.

12 large crimini mushrooms (1½ inch caps)

Olive oil

Salt and freshly ground black pepper

2 strips of bacon, chopped

1 cup minced stemmed swiss chard

1 garlic clove, minced

½ cup requesón or ricotta

1 Preheat the oven to 350°F.

2 Stem the mushrooms and chop the stems. Set aside. Toss the mushroom caps in a large bowl with 1 tablespoon olive oil, ½ teaspoon salt, and ¼ teaspoon pepper. Transfer the caps to a baking sheet, cavity side up. Bake for 15 minutes, until the cavities fill with liquid. Remove from the oven and let cool slightly. Discard any liquid in the mushrooms and on the pan. Return the mushrooms to the baking sheet.

3 Cook the bacon in a medium skillet over medium heat, stirring, until crisp, about 6 minutes. Transfer to paper towels to drain; reserve the pan drippings. Add the chopped mushroom stems to the drippings and sauté until tender, about 5 minutes. Add the chard and garlic and sauté until the chard wilts, about 3 minutes. Turn off the heat and stir in the cheese and bacon. Season with salt and pepper.

4 Stuff the mushroom caps with the chard mixture, dividing equally. Return to the oven and bake until heated through, 10 minutes.

arroz rojo

serves 4 to 6

2 plum tomatoes, cored

2 tablespoons vegetable oil

1 cup minced white onion

2 garlic cloves, minced

1 cup long-grain rice

¼ cup canned tomato sauce

1¾ cups chicken broth, preferably organic

1 serrano chile

1 sprig cilantro

Salt

I'M ALMOST CERTAIN THAT EVERY HOME across Mexico has its version of this tomato-tinted rice dish. My mom would make this in large quantities because it was mandatory at the dinner table almost every day of the week. Although I'm not the biggest fan of the microwave, my mom had this great trick for reheating the rice that would keep it nice and moist: Drench a paper towel with water, then squeeze out the excess, and cover the bowl of cold rice before popping it in the microwave. This creates a little steam so the rice doesn't dry out.

1 Using a box grater, grate the tomatoes into a medium bowl.

2 Heat the oil over medium-high heat in a heavy medium skillet. Add the onion and sauté until translucent, 5 minutes. Add the garlic and cook for 1 minute. Stir in the rice and cook until slightly toasted, about 3 minutes.

3 Add the grated tomato, tomato sauce, and broth and bring to a boil. Add the serrano, cilantro, and salt to taste. Bring to a boil, reduce the heat to medium, and simmer until the liquid is absorbed and the rice is tender, about 15 minutes.

4 Remove the skillet from the heat. Cover the rice and let stand for 8 minutes. Fluff the rice with a fork, transfer to a serving bowl, and serve.

leftovers?

rice and chicken soup: Add Arroz Rojo to chicken broth along with some cut-up veggies and shredded chicken for a hearty soup.

red rice gratin: Spoon rice into a gratin dish and top with Mexican crema or sour cream and mozzarella cheese. Bake at 350°F until the cheese is golden brown.

FOIL-WRAPPED **onions**

serves 6

1 cup Worcestershire sauce

1 cup Maggi seasoning sauce
(see Note, page 40)

6 tablespoons fresh lime juice

1½ teaspoons salt

6 large white onions

12 small yellow chiles

WRAPPING AND ROASTING ONIONS allows them to caramelize and brown but stay incredibly moist. The Maggi seasoning is a must; you can find it in Mexican markets and most supermarkets. Keep the onions in their foil packets so you don't lose any of their juices, and serve with tacos or carne asada. I also like to lightly season halibut, throw it on the grill, and then top with the onions and the chiles.

1 Preheat the oven to 350°F.

2 Mix the Worcestershire sauce, Maggi sauce, lime juice, and salt in a large bowl. Peel and quarter the onions, leaving the root ends together so the layers won't fall apart while cooking. Toss the onions and chiles in the marinade until well coated. Let sit for 10 minutes.

3 Cut twelve 6-inch squares of aluminum foil. Put 6 pieces of foil on a flat work surface and top each with another piece of foil for double wrapping. Place 2 chiles in the center of each piece of foil and top each chile with 4 onion wedges. Fold up the foil of each packet to form a cup. Divide the marinade remaining in the bowl among the foil packages. Enclose the onions tightly with foil and transfer to a rimmed baking sheet.

4 Roast until the onions are caramelized and the chiles are tender, about 1 hour. Let cool for 10 minutes. Open the packages slightly before serving.

caramelized yams WITH MARSHMALLOW AND STREUSEL

1½ pounds small yams, peeled and halved lengthwise

¾ cup almonds, coarsely chopped

5 ounces Maria cookies (about 32) or graham crackers (about 18)

1 teaspoon ground cinnamon

½ teaspoon salt

6 tablespoons (¾ stick) unsalted butter, chilled, diced, plus more for the dish

6 firm-ripe bananas, peeled and halved lengthwise

1 (10.5-ounce) bag mini marshmallows

IS THIS A DESSERT OR A SIDE? Well, that depends on what side of the border you're on. At my house, this comes out with dessert, but on the U.S. side this is an accompaniment to turkey. Whenever you serve it, it's superb. With checkered layers of yam and banana and a streusel topping that comes out crunchy when the marshmallows melt and caramelize, it will quickly become one of your holiday faves. For best results, the bananas and the yams should be similar in size.

1 Put the yams in a heavy medium pot and cover with cold water. Bring to a boil over high heat. Reduce the heat and simmer the yams until tender, about 10 minutes. The color of the yams will turn brighter and a knife will be able to pierce them easily.

2 Meanwhile put the almonds, cookies, cinnamon, and salt in a food processor and pulse a few times to combine until coarse, not fully ground. Add the butter and pulse a few times until the mixture comes together. Transfer the mixture to a large bowl and, working quickly, rub the mixture between your fingers until the streusel is in lumps slightly larger than peas. Refrigerate the streusel until ready to use.

3 Preheat the oven to 375°F. Grease the bottom of a 9 × 13-inch baking glass dish with butter.

4 Spread half of the bananas and yams in one layer in the bottom of the dish. Sprinkle with half of the streusel and half of the marshmallows. Repeat with the remaining ingredients to make one more layer. Bake for 25 minutes or until the marshmallows are golden. Serve warm.

salsas

salsas can make or break a dish. A simple cheese quesadilla can become something entirely special when served with sweet-tart Roasted Apple and Tomatillo Salsa (page 143). Spooning on some drop-dead gorgeous Pomegranate, Basil, and Queso Fresco Salsa (page 151) will take a grilled halibut fillet to a totally different level. Or just put out a bowl of Pecan and Chile de Árbol Salsa (page 144) with warm tortilla chips and watch your guests or family devour it before you get a chance to sit down.

If smoky, rich tastes are your thing, go for the salsas made from dried chiles. A good tip is to put the dried chile at the tip of your tongue to taste for spiciness before cooking with it so you'll know what you're in for. For brighter flavors, try the fresh salsas. Salsas made from roasted ingredients get a little sweetness from the caramelization in the oven. You'll find a salsa for every palate in this chapter!

easy chipotle MAYO

I LOVE MAYO—ON EVERYTHING. Especially on tostadas or tortas or burgers or grilled corn or . . . I always have a batch of this mayo on hand in the fridge. A ham and cheese sandwich jumps to a whole new level with a smear of spicy, smoky chipotle mayo. For a spicy kick, stir some into your potato salad, tuna salad, or coleslaw.

In a small bowl, mash together the chipotle chiles, lime juice, mayonnaise, and cilantro. Season with salt and pepper.

makes ½ cup

2 canned chipotle chiles in adobo sauce

2 teaspoons fresh lime juice

½ cup mayonnaise

1 tablespoon chopped fresh cilantro

Salt and freshly ground black pepper

roasted apple and tomatillo
SALSA

makes 3½ cups

THIS IS CURRENTLY MY FAVORITE SALSA! The unexpected addition of apples makes for a great texture and adds to the sweetness of roasted tomatillos. I also like to add some diced fresh apple right at the end, for freshness and crunch. Take a flour quesadilla, add some sliced avocados, and top with this salsa. Perfection.

1 Preheat the oven to 375°F.

2 Put the tomatillos, 2 of the apples, the onion, garlic, and jalapeño on a rimmed baking sheet. Toss with the olive oil and season with salt and pepper. Roast until tomatillos are softened and slightly charred, about 20 minutes.

3 Peel the garlic, then transfer all of the ingredients to a blender and puree until smooth. Season with salt and pepper.

4 Chop the remaining apple into ¼-inch cubes and stir into the salsa before serving.

1 pound tomatillos, husked and rinsed

3 green apples, such as Granny Smith, quartered

½ medium white onion

3 garlic cloves, unpeeled

1 jalapeño chile, stemmed

2 tablespoons olive oil

Salt and freshly ground black pepper

pecan and chile de árbol
SALSA

makes ½ cup

¼ **cup pecans**

4 chiles de árbol, stemmed

1 whole garlic clove

¼ **cup water**

Salt and freshly ground black pepper

I WAS AT AN EVENT AT MY SON'S SCHOOL recently when my childhood friend Karina Ruiz told me about this wonderful pecan and chile de árbol salsa she had tried while in Mexico City. She didn't have the recipe, but after asking her about the consistency, spiciness, and color, we came up with this wonderful table salsa that would be superb over a char-grilled steak.

1 Heat a heavy medium skillet over medium-high heat. Add the pecans and toast, tossing occasionally. until fragrant and lightly browned, about 3 minutes. Transfer the pecans to a plate.

2 Add the chiles and garlic to the dry skillet and toast until golden on all sides, 2 minutes. Transfer to a blender. Add the pecans and water, and blend until smooth. Season with salt and pepper.

leftovers?

pecan chicken tacos: Add shredded cooked chicken to the salsa and serve with warm corn tortillas for soft tacos.

cream of pecan soup: Warm the salsa in a medium saucepan, then add equal parts chicken broth and heavy cream until you have a soup. Boil until slightly thickened. Season with salt and pepper. Garnish with crumbled tortilla chips.

pasilla-guajillo SALSA

3 dried pasilla chiles

3 dried guajillo chiles

3 garlic cloves

2 cups warm water

Salt and freshly ground black pepper

PASILLAS GIVE THIS SALSA A RICH FLAVOR while most of the kick comes from the guajillo. The salsa, which comes out looking like a puree, is what I use mostly to season broths or soups (like the Beef Pozole on page 58). If you thin it a little bit with either chicken or vegetable broth, it's a superb sauce for enchiladas or chilaquiles.

Soak the pasillas, guajillos, and garlic in the warm water until the chiles are soft, about 10 minutes. Pour into a blender and process until smooth. Season salt and pepper.

tomatillo and chile de árbol
SALSA

makes 1½ cups

FOR SOFT AND SLIGHTLY SWEET CORN TAMALES (page 193), this pan-roasted salsa is the perfect counterpoint. When making roasted tomatillo salsas, fresh jalapeños or serranos are usually used, but I love the flavor of toasted chile de árbol and the bright red specks it gives the salsa.

1 In a large sauté pan, heat the olive oil over medium-high heat. Add the tomatillos, onion, garlic, and chiles. Cook for about 7 minutes, until the tomatillo skins are browned.

2 Carefully peel the garlic cloves and add to the blender along with the tomatillos, onion, and chiles. Add the cilantro and water. Process until smooth, about 2 minutes. Season with salt and pepper.

1 tablespoon olive oil

8 tomatillos, husked and rinsed (about 1 pound)

½ white white onion

2 garlic cloves, unpeeled

3 chiles de árbol, stemmed, seeded, and torn into pieces

2 tablespoons chopped fresh cilantro

1 cup water

Salt and freshly ground black pepper

salsa asada

makes 2 cups

8 plum tomatoes, cored

1 large shallot, peeled

2 serrano chiles, stemmed

⅓ cup chicken broth, preferably organic

Salt and freshly ground black pepper

OF ALL THE SALSAS IN THIS BOOK, this is the most traditional in terms of preparation. The term *asado* can refer to grilled or dry-pan roasted, as I do with this salsa. Cooking in a dry skillet allows the ingredients to char so you get that nice, smoky flavor. Where I do break from tradition is in using a more mildly flavored shallot, but you can make it with white onion instead.

Heat a heavy medium skillet over medium-high heat. Add the tomatoes, shallot, and serranos and roast in the dry skillet until golden brown on all sides, about 8 minutes. Transfer to a blender, add the broth, and blend until smooth. Season with salt and pepper.

pomegranate, basil, and queso fresco SALSA

THIS IS A SALSA, but whenever I make it I just end up eating it by the spoonful like a salad. The combination of the tart, crisp pomegranate, creamy cheese, and crunchy pine nuts makes a wonderful topping for grilled fish or even a carne asada taco. Pine nuts can be expensive because of the labor-intensive work of extracting them from the pine cones, plus they have a high fat content, which makes them turn rancid quickly. So buy a small quantity and store them in the fridge for no longer than three months.

¼ cup pine nuts

Seeds from 1 large pomegranate (about 1 cup)

2 tablespoons thinly sliced fresh basil

2 tablespoons crumbled queso fresco or feta

1 teaspoon olive oil

Salt and freshly ground black pepper

1 Toast the pine nuts in a dry skillet over medium heat until golden, 4 minutes. Transfer to a plate to cool.

2 In a small bowl, mix the pomegranate seeds, basil, queso fresco, and cooled pine nuts. Drizzle with the olive oil and season with salt and pepper.

GRILLED CORN **pico de gallo**

makes 3 cups

1 ear of corn

1½ pounds ripe tomatoes, seeded and chopped

¾ cup chopped onion

½ cup chopped fresh cilantro

3 tablespoons fresh lime juice

2 serrano chiles, stemmed, seeded, and minced

Salt and freshly ground black pepper

HERE, THE TRADITIONAL PICO DE GALLO SALSA gets the addition of some natural sweetness and crunch from grilled fresh corn. When taking the kernels off of the cob, I always like to place a kitchen towel on my work surface so the kernels don't fly around all over the place. It also makes them easy to transport from board to bowl. Use this summer salsa for Chicken Flautas (page 28), grilled chicken, or quesadillas. If corn is out of season, leave it out and you'll have a perfect simple salsa for tortilla chips.

1 Heat a dry grill pan over medium-high heat. Grill the corn, turning occasionally, until darkened in spots, about 10 minutes. Set aside until it is cool enough to handle.

2 Using a sharp knife, carefully cut the kernels off the cobs and add them to a medium bowl. Mix in the tomatoes, onion, cilantro, lime juice, and serrano. Season with salt and pepper. Cover and chill for at least 30 minutes, until flavors blend. (The salsa can be made up to 4 hours ahead.)

spicy tomato BROTH

makes 4½ cups

SALSA CAN COME IN MANY DIFFERENT TEXTURES; this one is actually a broth. Usually used more as a sauce (like for the chiles rellenos; page 98) this sauce can also be drizzled on flautas (page 28) or tostadas (page 81). Stir it into soups to add a little bit of richness and spice.

6 plum tomatoes, cored

1 small white onion, peeled and quartered

2 garlic cloves

½ teaspoon dried oregano, preferably Mexican, crumbled

3 cups chicken broth, preferably organic

Salt and freshly ground black pepper

Combine the tomatoes, onion, garlic, and oregano in a blender and process until smooth. Transfer to a heavy medium saucepan and the add broth. Bring to a boil over medium-high heat. Reduce the heat and simmer until bright red, about 10 minutes. Season with salt and pepper.

desserts

flan is what most people conjure up when they think of Mexican desserts, and I love it with a little twist—in my recipe (page 159), the flan gets a kick from coconut. But there's so much more to Mexican desserts! We've got wine country in Baja and what better way to highlight those flavors than in Figs in Red Wine and Honey (page 167)? And then there's Mexican chocolate, flavored with almond and cinnamon, and the secret to some of my favorite desserts. It's the star in my Mexican Chocolate Pecan Pie (page 163), which my mother was obsessed with, and Mexican Chocolate Bread Pudding (page 160).

These desserts are meant to inspire and expand your repertoire of Mexican sweets. My goal in life is for every home in America to have Mexican chocolate and a jar of creamy, rich, caramely cajeta in the pantry next to the cinnamon and graham crackers!

maria cookie
AND LIME CREAM TRIFLE

serves 6 to 8

THERE ARE TOO MANY DESSERTS made with sweetened condensed milk in Mexico to count, so it's saying a lot that this is one of my favorites. You need only a couple of ingredients, and if you don't have a trifle mold, any glass baking dish will work. Maria cookies, the Mexican version of the English tea biscuit, are a little firmer than graham crackers so they stand up well to the cream, but you could use either.

2 (14-ounce) cans sweetened condensed milk

2 (12-ounce) cans evaporated milk

2/3 cup fresh lime juice (from 5 limes)

2 (5.5-ounce) packages Maria cookies or 2 (4.8-ounce) packages graham crackers

1 Blend the condensed milk, evaporated milk, and lime juice in a blender until smooth.

2 Spoon ½ cup of the lime cream into the bottom of a 12-cup glass trifle dish. Arrange one-third of the crackers over the cream, breaking them as needed to form a single layer. Spread 1 cup of the cream over the crackers. Repeat twice to make to more layers, ending with a layer of cream. Chill, covered tightly with plastic wrap, until set, at least 2 hours, or overnight. Bring to room temperature before serving.

coconut FLAN

FLAN (WHICH, I HAVE TO CONFESS, IS SPANISH, NOT MEXICAN) is surprisingly easy to make. The trick is to cook it in a water bath to ensure gentle heat surrounds the custard so it won't break or curdle. There are various methods of infusing coconut flavor into a flan, but coconut milk is the easiest, giving you intense flavor and also a smooth texture. When I first made this recipe, I thought adding shredded coconut to custard would give even more flavor. It does, but it takes away from the velvety texture, so I opt to sprinkle some toasted coconut on the top instead.

1 Preheat the oven to 350°F. Spray a Bundt pan with cooking spray and drizzle the cajeta into the pan, turning to coat the bottom and sides.

2 Using an electric mixer, beat the condensed milk, coconut milk, evaporated milk, eggs, vanilla, and salt. Pour the mixture over the cajeta into the Bundt pan. Put the pan inside a roasting pan and fill the roasting pan with warm water to come halfway up the sides of the Bundt pan. Cover the Bundt pan with foil.

3 Bake until the center jiggles slightly when the pan is moved, about 1 hour 40 minutes. Remove from the oven and let cool for 30 minutes, then transfer to the refrigerator and chill for 3 hours or overnight.

4 Turn the flan out onto a platter. Sprinkle with toasted coconut and serve.

serves 8 to 10

Nonstick cooking spray

1 cup cajeta or caramel sauce, warm

3 (14-ounce) cans sweetened condensed milk

1 (14-ounce) can unsweetened coconut milk

1 (14-ounce) can evaporated milk

6 large eggs

1 tablespoon pure vanilla extract

½ teaspoon salt

½ cup shredded sweetened coconut, toasted

mexican chocolate
BREAD PUDDING

serves 6 to 8

5 cups cubed (1½ inch) stale bolillo rolls (about 3; see Note, page 46) or baguette

2¾ cups whole milk

4 ounces Mexican or bittersweet chocolate, chopped

1 cup granulated sugar

3 large egg yolks

2 large eggs

⅓ cup raisins

1 tablespoon ground cinnamon

1 tablespoon unsalted butter

Confectioners' sugar

INSPIRED BY THE TRADITIONAL DESSERT from Michoacán known as *capirotada*, this bread pudding is drenched in cinnamony Mexican chocolate. Stale bread is key because, even though you want the custard to be fully absorbed, you don't want the bread pieces to fall apart. If you don't have stale bread, just leave the cut-up pieces in your (turned-off) oven overnight to dry out. Dust with plenty of powdered sugar at the end and serve with Mexican Hot Chocolate (page 207).

1 Put the bread cubes in a large bowl. Bring the milk just to simmer in a large heavy saucepan. Remove from the heat, add the chocolate, and whisk until melted and smooth.

2 Whisk together the sugar, eggs, and egg yolks in a medium bowl. Gradually add the chocolate mixture into the egg mixture, whisking constantly. Stir in the raisins and cinnamon. Pour the custard over the bread cubes. Let stand until most of the custard is absorbed, about 1 hour.

3 Preheat the oven to 350°F. Butter an 8-inch baking dish.

4 Pour the bread and custard into the prepared dish. Bake the bread pudding until just set but the center moves slightly when the dish is shaken, 45 minutes. Serve warm or at room temperature dusted with confectioners' sugar.

mexican chocolate pecan PIE

serves 8 to 10

MY MOTHER WAS OBSESSED WITH PECAN PIE so I decided to whip up a recipe using Mexican chocolate. I always like to top this with a cinnamon-spiced whipped cream or a little vanilla ice cream.

Nonstick cooking spray

1½ cups graham cracker or Maria cookie crumbs

12 tablespoons (1½ sticks) unsalted butter, plus 7 tablespoons, melted

½ cup plus 2 tablespoons (packed) light brown sugar

6 tablespoons light corn syrup

3 cups pecan halves

¼ cup Mexican crema or heavy cream

1 disc Mexican chocolate or 3 ounces bittersweet chocolate, finely chopped

1 Spray a 9-inch pie dish with cooking spray.

2 Process the cookie crumbs, 7 tablespoons melted butter, and 2 tablespoons of the brown sugar in a food processor until the crumbs are moist. Press the crumb mixture into the bottom and up the sides of the pie dish. Cover and freeze while preparing the filling (or for up to 1 week).

3 Preheat the oven to 350°F.

4 Combine the 12 tablespoons butter, remaining ½ cup brown sugar, and the corn syrup in a heavy medium saucepan. Bring to a boil over medium-high heat, stirring often. Boil for 1 minute. Stir in the pecans and crema. Boil until the mixture thickens slightly, about 3 minutes. Remove from the heat, add the chocolate, and stir until melted and smooth.

4 Pour the hot filling into the crust. Using a spoon, evenly distribute the nuts. Bake until the filling bubbles all over, about 15 minutes. Transfer the pie to a rack and cool completely before serving.

pineapple-cajeta
EMPANADAS

serves 8 to 10

Nonstick cooking spray

1 (1-pound) package frozen puff pastry, thawed

All-purpose flour

¼ cup cajeta or caramel sauce

½ cup grated Monterey Jack cheese

1 cup cubed (½ inch) fresh pineapple

2 large eggs, beaten with 1 tablespoon water

2 tablespoons demarara sugar or raw sugar

THESE ARE ADDICTIVE. No matter what size batch you make, they will disappear. To make an empanada, you usually have to make the dough, which can be a hassle. I like to use purchased puff pastry instead. Press the empanadas tightly to enclose the filling so the cajeta doesn't seep out during baking. This is one of those recipes that I love to involve Fausto in. If you don't have round molds, just used a cleaned-out can of tuna to cut the circles.

1 Preheat the oven to 350°F. Coat a large baking sheet with cooking spray.

2 Unfold one sheet of puff pastry on a lightly floured surface. Using a floured rolling pin, roll out to a ¼-inch thickness. Using a 3-inch round cutter or inverted glass, cut out 9 circles. Repeat with the remaining puff pastry sheet. Spoon a scant teaspoon of cajeta in the center of each round.

3 Top each with a sprinkling of grated cheese and 3 or 4 pieces of pineapple. Brush the edge of each circle with egg wash and fold each empanada into a half-moon. Crimp the edges with a fork.

4 Transfer the empanadas to the prepared baking sheet and brush them with the remaining egg wash. Sprinkle the empanadas with demarara sugar and bake until golden brown, about 30 minutes. Serve warm.

bananas tequila foster

serves 4

4 medium ripe but firm bananas

2 tablespoons orange juice

4 tablespoons sugar

4 tablespoons (½ stick) unsalted butter

¼ teaspoon ground cinnamon

¼ cup añejo tequila

1 pint vanilla ice cream

PEDRO HUERTA, THE AMAZING COOK who fed my family for many years while I was growing up in Mexico, used to make this for us all of the time. He would usually save it for special occasions, though, like birthdays or when my dad had friends over for dinner. He would put on a show for us with the flambé, but if you're not feeling particularly brave, just add the alcohol, bring to a boil, and cook for a few minutes. You just want the alcohol to cook off, which you can a achieve with a quick boil.

1 Peel the bananas and slice in half lengthwise. Brush with 1 tablespoon of the orange juice and sprinkle with 2 tablespoons of the sugar.

2 Melt the butter with the remaining 2 tablespoons sugar in a heavy large skillet. Add the bananas and sauté until just tender, about 1 minute. Sprinkle with the cinnamon.

3 Add the tequila and remaining 1 tablespoon orange juice, and cook for 2 minutes. Remove from the heat. Scoop ice cream into bowls and put bananas over ice cream and serve.

leftovers?

boozy banana pancakes: Cut cooked bananas into 1-inch cubes and add to pancake batter before making pancakes. Reheat the sauce and use to top the pancakes along with a little butter.

banana rolls: Fill store-bought spring roll wrappers with the warm bananas. Fry in 350°F vegetable oil until golden brown and serve with whipped cream for dipping.

banana, tequila, and coffee trifles: Mix a little strong coffee into some whipped cream and layer in glasses with the cooked bananas and graham cracker crumbs for easy individual trifles.

figs IN RED WINE AND HONEY

serves 4

2 cups dry red wine

¼ cup honey

1 tablespoon sugar

1 (3-inch) cinnamon stick

8 mission figs (firm but ripe), stemmed and halved lengthwise

½ cup evaporated milk

THERE WAS A HUGE FIG TREE IN THE BACKYARD of my aunt Laura's house in Tijuana, and I vividly remember climbing that tree with my cousins Coque and Christian, picking and biting into the sweetest figs, which really don't need any cooking or added flavors when picked off the tree and perfectly sweet! But we don't all have fig trees in our backyards, and so this wine-based syrup ensures a simply delicious dessert. Evaporated milk is drizzled over the figs at the end to enrich the syrup and, when mixed in, make it smooth and creamy.

1   In a nonreactive medium saucepan, combine the wine, honey, sugar, and cinnamon stick. Bring to a simmer over medium heat and simmer for 20 minutes, until slightly thickened.

2   Add the figs and simmer for 30 minutes, until the mixture is thick and reduced.

3   Divide the figs among 4 small bowls. Drizzle with the evaporated milk and serve.

leftovers?

baked brie: Top a round of brie with the cooked fig mixture and bake at 375°F until the cheese is soft.

drunken fig marmalade: Puree half of the cooked fig mixture and mix back into the other half. Serve with toast and butter for breakfast. Or stir in chopped fresh thyme and use as a savory-sweet topping for roasted chicken breasts.

fig and goat cheese crostata: Roll a sheet of defrosted store-bought puff pastry into a 9-inch round. Spread with herbed fresh goat cheese and top with the figs, leaving a 2-inch border. Fold the border partially over the filling. Bake at 350°F until golden.

requesón CHEESECAKE

serves 6 to 8

2 4.8-ounce packages cinnamon-sugar graham crackers (18 crackers)

8 tablespoons (1 stick) unsalted butter, melted

1 (8-ounce) package cream cheese, at room temperature

1 (14-ounce) can sweetened condensed milk

15 ounces fresh requesón or ricotta cheese

1 tablespoon pure vanilla extract

1 teaspoon grated orange zest

4 large eggs

Apple-Cranberry Compote (recipe follows; optional)

REQUESÓN IS THE MEXICAN VERSION OF RICOTTA, and just like ricotta, it is used in both sweet and savory dishes. Because it's combined with cream cheese here, versus the traditional cheesecake that's all cream cheese, the custard comes out puffed and airy. A great tip for this (or any other) cheesecake is to place a small metal bowl of water in the oven alongside the pan to create steam while you bake, which will keep your cheesecake from cracking.

1 Preheat the oven to 350°F.

2 Put the graham crackers in the bowl of a food processor and process to crumbs (about 2 cups). Add the butter and process until well combined. Pat the crumbs into the bottom and 1½ inches up the sides of a 9-inch springform pan. Put the pan on a baking sheet and bake the crust until golden, about 10 minutes. Let cool completely on a wire rack, about 25 minutes. Leave the oven on.

3 In the bowl of an electric mixer, beat the cream cheese and condensed milk until smooth and pale, then beat in the requesón, vanilla, and zest until smooth. Add the eggs, one at a time, beating well after each addition. Pour the custard into the cooled crust.

4 Bake until the cheesecake is puffed and golden and a tester inserted 1 inch from the center comes out clean, about 50 minutes. Let cool on a rack at room temperature for 35 minutes. Cover with plastic wrap and refrigerate for at least 2 hours or overnight. Bring to room temperature before serving.

5 Top the cheesecake with the compote, if desired, before serving.

apple-cranberry compote

makes 1 cup

In a medium heavy skillet, melt the butter over medium heat. Add the sugar and cook until thickened, about 4 minutes. Add the apples, cranberries, and cinnamon and cook, stirring occasionally, until the apples are tender and cranberries are plump, about 8 minutes. Cool to room temperature.

4 tablespoons (½ stick) unsalted butter

¼ cup (packed) dark brown sugar

2 Granny Smith apples, peeled, cored, and cut into ½-inch pieces

¼ cup dried cranberries

¼ teaspoon ground cinnamon

chocolate-mint POTS DE CRÈME

serves 4

1¼ cups heavy cream

⅔ cup whole milk

½ cup fresh mint leaves, chopped

6 ounces bittersweet chocolate, finely chopped

1 teaspoon pure vanilla extract

6 large egg yolks

3 tablespoons sugar

2 tablespoons dark rum

I LOVE THE TASTE OF SWEET RUM and bittersweet chocolate together. Bake the custards in colorful, ovenproof tea cups or ramekins, and serve with a dollop of whipped cream.

1 Preheat the oven to 300°F.

2 Bring the cream and milk to a simmer in heavy medium saucepan over medium heat. Remove the pan from the heat. Add the mint leaves, cover, and steep for 10 minutes.

3 Put the chocolate in a large bowl. Strain the cream mixture into the chocolate and stir until completely melted. Whisk together the egg yolks, sugar, and rum in another large bowl. Gradually whisk the warm cream mixture into the yolk mixture, then strain. Let stand for 2 minutes. Whisk until the custard is smooth.

3 Divide the custard among four 1-cup ramekins or custard cups. Arrange the ramekins in a roasting pan and carefully add enough warm water to the pan to come halfway up the sides of the ramekins. Cover the roasting pan with aluminum foil. Bake the custards until just set in center, about 30 minutes. Remove the ramekins from the water, uncover, and refrigerate until cold, at least 6 hours or overnight.

strawberry rompope
SHAKE

2 cups fresh strawberries, hulled, plus more for serving

1 cup whole milk

2 pints strawberry ice cream, slightly softened

2 tablespoons sugar

½ cup Mexican rompope or eggnog

IT'S PRETTY REMARKABLE how many historic Mexican dishes and culinary contributions were developed by nuns in convents. Rompope, the Mexican version of rum-spiked eggnog, is one of them. So when do you serve a shake with a rum kick? At a grownup party, for sure, and alongside a burger, preferably Burgers al Pastor (page 72) and with some fries.

1 Put four 8-ounce glasses in the freezer for 1 hour.

2 Combine the strawberries, milk, 1 pint of the ice cream, and the sugar in a blender. Puree until smooth. Add the second pint of ice cream and rompope, and puree until almost smooth.

3 Divide the mixture among the frozen glasses. Garnish each with a strawberry, if desired, and serve with spoon and straw.

banana and cajeta layered CREPES

1 cup all-purpose flour

2 tablespoons sugar

½ cup plus 2 tablespoons water

½ cup whole milk

3 large eggs

2 tablespoons unsalted butter, melted, plus more for cooking

½ teaspoon salt

1 cup cajeta or caramel sauce

½ cup heavy cream

4 ounces cream cheese, at room temperature

5 large, firm but ripe bananas, sliced

1½ cups finely chopped pecans

CAJETA, CARAMELIZED GOAT'S MILK, is one of my favorite Mexican confections. It's addictive and a million times more flavorful and complex than regular caramel—though a thick one is a good substitution in a pinch. The goat's milk gives it its distinctive, slightly tangy flavor, making it much less cloying than plain caramel. Go for ripe but firm when picking the bananas so they don't turn to mush when you're layering them with the crepes.

1 Combine the flour, sugar, water, milk, eggs, butter, and salt in a blender and process until smooth, about 5 seconds. Turn off the motor, use a rubber spatula to scrape down the sides of the blender, and blend the batter for 20 seconds longer. Transfer to a bowl, cover, and let the batter stand for 1 hour. (The batter may be made 1 day ahead and kept in the refrigerator.)

2 Blend the cajeta, heavy cream, and cream cheese in a clean blender until smooth.

3 Select a crepe pan or nonstick skillet that measures 6 to 7 inches across the bottom. Heat over medium heat until it is hot. Brush the pan lightly with a little butter, and heat it until it is hot but not smoking. Stir the batter and pour ¼ cup batter into the pan. Tilt and rotate the pan quickly to cover the bottom with a thin layer of batter. Loosen the edge of the crepe with a spatula, and cook for 1 minute, or until the top appears almost dry. Turn the crepe, cook the other side lightly, about 20 seconds, and transfer to a plate. Continue making crepes with the remaining batter, brushing the pan lightly with butter as necessary and stacking the finished crepes on top of one another.

4 Pour ¼ cup of the cajeta cream into a 9-inch round glass dish. Top with one crepe, one-fifth each of the banana slices, pecans, and cream mixture. Repeat with the remaining crepes, bananas, pecans, and cream to make 5 layers, finishing with the pecans and cream. Cover and refrigerate until set, at least 45 minutes or up to 4 hours. Serve at room temperature.

breakfast
and brunch

forget cereal or doughnuts. There is nothing in the world like a good Mexican breakfast. Whether it's Huevos Rancheros (page 187) or Chicken and Tomatillo Enchilada Gratin (page 184), there's something about the addition of spicy salsas that just makes eggs and casseroles so much better. Scrambled Eggs with Crispy Tortillas (page 182), perfectly cooked fluffy eggs mixed with crisp salty tortilla triangles, take me right back to my aunt Laura's house.

For those who prefer something sweet at the start of the day, Cinnamon Pan Frances (page 196), a Mexican take on French toast, will hit the spot, as will soft Corn Tamales (page 193), which I'd eat any time of day, really.

quesadillas DRENCHED IN BEAN SAUCE

THIS ARE THE SIMPLEST OF *ENFRIJOLADAS,* or drenched-in-bean dishes.The quesadillas are stuffed just with cheese, but you could easily add cooked chorizo for more substance. Although we usually had these for breakfast, they are sometimes stuffed with shredded chicken along with the cheese and served as an early dinner, or *merienda,* in Mexico.

1 Preheat the oven to 350°F.

2 Put the beans and broth in a large bowl. Sprinkle the oregano over the bean mixture. Season with salt and pepper.

3 Heat the olive oil in a large sauté pan over medium-high heat. Add the chopped onion, tomato, serrano, and garlic. Sauté until the onion is soft, about 5 minutes. Add the beans and broth to the pan and bring to a simmer over medium-high heat. Simmer 10 minutes to blend the flavors.

4 Let cool slightly and then transfer to a blender and puree until smooth. Return the pureed mixture to the pan and keep hot over medium-low heat, stirring frequently.

5 Using tongs, pass the tortillas, one at a time, through the bean sauce until they are somewhat softened and coated on both sides with the sauce. Set aside on a plate. Fill each tortilla with ¼ cup shredded cheese. Fold them in half and arrange them, overlapping, in a 9 × 13-inch baking dish. Top with the remaining bean sauce.

6 Bake until the cheese is melted, 10 to 15 minutes. Drizzle with crema, sprinkle with red onion rings, and serve.

2 (15-ounce) cans pinto beans, rinsed and drained

3 cups chicken broth, preferably organic

½ teaspoon dried oregano, preferably Mexican, crumbled

Salt and freshly ground black pepper

1 tablespoon olive oil

¾ cup chopped white onion

1 plum tomato, roughly chopped

1 serrano chile, stemmed, seeded, and minced

2 garlic cloves, minced

8 (6-inch) corn tortillas

2 cups shredded Swiss or Monterey Jack cheese

¼ cup Mexican crema or sour cream

2 thin slices red onion, separated into rings

oven-roasted poblano and egg
CASSEROLES

serves 2

ONCE YOU'VE MASTERED CHARRING AND PEELING POBLANOS, you'll want to put them in everything you make! We have this ongoing joke on the *Mexican Made Easy* set about how I do this in every episode. That's not true, but I do love how the smell of charring them directly over a gas burner makes my kitchen smell so homey and comforting. Once you have your poblanos ready for this recipe, you just put everything in a baking dish and pop it in the oven.

1 Preheat the oven to 350°F.

2 Melt the butter in a small heavy skillet over medium-low heat. Add the onion and sauté until translucent, 5 minutes. Add the poblano strips and mushrooms, and cook until the liquid from the mushrooms evaporates, about 8 minutes. Season with salt and pepper.

3 Divide the poblano mixture between 2 individual ovenproof casserole dishes (see Note). Carefully crack 2 eggs into each one. Bake until the whites are just set, about 12 minutes for soft yolks or 15 minutes for slightly firm yolks.

4 Carefully remove the casseroles from the oven and sprinkle each with 2 tablespoons cheese. Return to the oven until the cheese melts, about 2 minutes. Serve in the casserole dishes, setting a plate under each one to protect your table.

2 tablespoons unsalted butter

¼ cup chopped white onion

¼ cup charred poblano strips (page 98)

½ cup sliced button mushrooms

Salt and freshly ground black pepper

4 large eggs

4 tablespoons shredded Monterey Jack cheese

NOTE If you don't have individual casserole dishes, use four 1-cup ramekins instead. Divide the poblano mixture them, top each one with 1 egg, and, once baked, sprinkle 1 tablespoon cheese over each serving.

scrambled eggs WITH
CRISPY TORTILLAS

4 large eggs

2 tablespoons Mexican crema or sour cream

Salt and freshly ground black pepper

2 tablespoons unsalted butter

2 tablespoons vegetable oil

4 (6-inch) corn tortillas, cut into ½-inch pieces

IT'S IRONIC THAT I OFTEN MENTION MY AUNT LAURA during my show, because the woman doesn't cook. She's got four or five go-to recipes that she's mastered, and I've ended up cooking those recipes some place or another. The reason for this, I think, is that I spent so much of my childhood at her house, and every morning she'd make the *exact* same breakfast, using the night-before's leftover tortillas—*migas,* or easy scrambled eggs with lightly fried tortilla chips, which I would drench in ketchup and sprinkle with tons of salt. Thanks, Aunt Laura, for both the memories and the recipes; as few as they are, they're great!

1 Whisk together the eggs, crema, and ½ teaspoon salt in a medium bowl.

2 Heat the butter and oil in a large heavy skillet over low heat. Add the tortillas and fry until crisp but not brown, about 8 minutes. Season lightly with salt.

3 Increase the heat to medium-high and add the egg mixture. Stir with a heatproof spatula until the eggs are almost set but still creamy, 4 to 5 minutes. Season with salt and pepper. Serve immediately.

chicken and tomatillo
ENCHILADA GRATIN

serves 4 to 6

9 tomatillos, husked and rinsed

¼ medium white onion

1 serrano chile

1 small yellow chile

2 garlic cloves

¼ bunch fresh cilantro

Salt and freshly ground black pepper

½ cup Mexican crema or sour cream

½ cup heavy cream

Vegetable oil

6 (6-inch) corn tortillas

1½ cups shredded cooked chicken

½ cup shredded Monterey Jack cheese

THESE ARE SAID TO HAVE BEEN BORN in a Mexico City restaurant called Cafe Imperial, in La Condesa, an area full of European immigrants. The chef there was serving a dinner for Austro-Hungarian royalty and thought of mixing some European cooking methods (gratin) with some Mexican ones (enchiladas). The result was *enchiladas suizas,* as this dish is known in Mexico. Before this, enchiladas were sprinkled with fresh cheese but never gratinéed.

1 Preheat the oven to 350°F.

2 Put the tomatillos, onion, serrano, and yellow chile in a heavy medium saucepan, cover with water, and bring to a boil over medium-high heat. Boil until the tomatillos turn olive-green color, about 10 minutes. Drain and transfer the tomatillos, onion, and chiles to a blender. Add the garlic and cilantro, and blend until smooth. Season with salt and pepper.

3 Mix the crema and heavy cream and season with salt.

4 Heat 1 tablespoon of oil in a small skillet over medium-high heat. Fry the tortillas, one at a time, until golden but still pliable, about 10 seconds per side. Transfer to paper towels to drain.

5 Put the tortillas on a work surface. Divide the shredded chicken evenly among the tortillas and roll up each like a cigar. Spread ⅓ cup sauce in a 9 × 13-inch glass baking dish. Arrange the enchiladas, seam side down, in one layer snugly in the dish. Pour the rest of the sauce over the enchiladas. Drizzle the cream mixture on top and sprinkle the cheese all over.

6 Bake until the cheese melts and starts to brown in spots, about 30 minutes. Serve immediately.

huevos rancheros

serves 2

2 tablespoons canola oil

4 (6-inch) corn tortillas

4 large eggs

Salt and freshly ground black pepper

Salsa Asada (page 148), warm

THERE'S NOT MUCH TO EXPLAIN ABOUT HUEVOS RANCHEROS, as they've now become an almost mainstream American breakfast. What I would suggest is that you try serving them *divorciados*, or divorced, sometime. This means topping each sunny-side up egg in a different colored salsa: one red and one green (you can use the Tomatillo and Chile de Árbol Salsa on page 147).

1 Heat 1 tablespoon of the oil in a medium nonstick skillet over medium heat. Add the tortillas, one at a time, and cook until crisp-tender, 30 seconds per side. Remove the tortillas to a piece of aluminum foil and wrap tightly to keep warm.

2 Heat the remaining 1 tablespoon oil in the same skillet and fry the eggs until just set, about 3 minutes. Sprinkle with salt and pepper.

3 Unwrap the tortillas and arrange them flat on 2 serving plates (2 tortillas per plate). Top each tortilla with a fried egg and spoon about ⅓ cup warm sauce on top. Serve immediately.

chipotle CHILAQUILES

serves 6

3 tablespoons canola oil

10 plum tomatoes, cored and quartered

1 small white onion

2 garlic cloves, unpeeled

2 canned chipotle chiles in adobo sauce, minced

Salt and freshly ground black pepper

16 (6-inch) corn tortillas, each cut into 8 wedges

¼ crumbled queso fresco or feta

¼ cup Mexican crema or sour cream

CHILAQUILES ARE BASICALLY TORTILLA CHIPS IN SALSA. More often they are prepared with a tomatillo-based green salsa, but this chipotle-based red salsa gives your chilaquiles a nice kick. As for the tortillas, there's never any reason to throw one out (unless it's green). I imagine, a long time ago, a frugal cook in Mexico with a bunch of stale tortillas (that he had probably made by hand) came up with this dish. That said, as stale as those tortillas may be, they don't hold their shape for too long in the salsa, so chilaquiles can't be made in advance. You can prep the salsa and chips the night before, but don't cook them together until you're ready to serve.

1 Preheat the oven to 400°F.

2 Heat the oil in a large heavy skillet over medium-high heat. Add the tomatoes, onion, and garlic and cook, turning frequently, until golden brown on all sides, about 10 minutes. Add the chipotles and cook for 1 minute. Transfer to a blender, add 1 tablespoon salt and 1 teaspoon pepper, and process until smooth.

3 Return the sauce to the skillet and cook over medium-low heat for 5 minutes. Season with salt and pepper, if needed. Turn off the heat and keep warm.

4 Arrange the tortilla wedges on baking sheets lined with parchment paper, spreading apart the tortillas. Bake until the tortilla chips are golden brown and crisp, about 10 minutes. Remove the chips from the oven and sprinkle with salt.

5 Stir the warm tortilla chips into the warm salsa in the skillet. Divide the mixture among plates. Sprinkle with queso fresco and drizzle with crema, dividing equally. Serve immediately.

open-faced bean and cheese
SANDWICHES

serves 4

MY SISTER, WHO'S BEEN KNOWN TO SURVIVE FOR DAYS on sweets alone, will dabble into the savories for this dish any day of the week. Fluffy bolillos—Mexican rolls with a crisp crust and a fluffy interior—topped with hearty beans, then gratinéed and topped with a fresh salsa make for a prefect breakfast or light lunch.

1 Preheat a broiler.

2 Heat the oil in a heavy medium skillet over medium heat. Add the onion and sauté until the onion is translucent, about 5 minutes. Add the garlic and cook for 1 minute. Add the beans, and using a potato masher, mash them until they resemble lumpy mashed potatoes. Season with salt and pepper.

3 Split the rolls lengthwise and put them on a baking sheet. Broil until lightly golden, about 3 minutes. Spread each half of the rolls with about ½ cup of the beans. Top with the shredded cheese.

4 Return to the oven and broil until the cheese is melted and starting to bubble. Transfer to plates, and serve with salsa.

2 tablespoons olive oil

½ cup chopped onion

1 garlic clove, minced

2 (15-ounce) cans pinto beans, rinsed and drained

Salt and freshly ground black pepper

4 bolillo rolls (see Note, page 46), or 1 baguette, cut into 4 pieces

1½ cups shredded Monterey Jack cheese

Roasted Apple and Tomatillo Salsa (page 143)

cowboy BEANS

serves 6

2 cups dried pinto beans

1 ham hock

1 bay leaf

3 garlic cloves

1 jalapeño chile

5 cups cold water

2 slices thick-cut bacon, chopped

⅔ cup finely chopped white onion

4 ounces raw chorizo, casing removed

Salt and freshly ground black pepper

A *CHARRO* IS A MEXICAN COWBOY—the really brave kind who jumps from bareback horse to bareback horse just to please a crowd. Fausto's dad, Fausto, is a charro, so I've witnessed this beautiful sport firsthand and know how difficult and strenuous it is to get through one of those grueling days in the *lienzo charro,* or ring. A substantial bean-based dish such as this one is often eaten by the cowboys before the competition begins.

1 Soak the beans overnight in enough cold water to cover them by at least 2 inches. Drain well.

2 Bring the beans, ham hock, bay leaf, garlic cloves, jalapeño, and cold water to a boil in a large heavy pot over high heat. Reduce the heat to medium and simmer until the beans are tender, about 2 hours. The beans should always be soupy. If they absorb too much water, add 1 cup water after 1 hour and continue cooking. Turn off the heat.

3 Cook the bacon in a large sauté pan over medium-high heat until almost crisp, about 10 minutes. Add the onion and sauté until onion is translucent, 5 minutes. Scoop the mixture into the pot with the beans.

4 Wipe the pan clean. Cook the chorizo over medium heat in the same pan until crisp, about 10 minutes. Using a slotted spoon, transfer the chorizo to paper towels to drain and then add to the beans.

5 Season the beans lightly with salt, if necessary, and pepper. Stir over medium-high heat for a few minutes, until heated through. Serve hot in a soup bowl.

corn TAMALES

serves 8 to 10

20 dried corn husks (see Note, page 195)

7 cups fresh corn kernels (from 7 ears of corn)

12 tablespoons (1½ sticks) unsalted butter, at room temperature

½ cup sugar

1 large egg

1½ teaspoons salt

1½ teaspoons baking powder

½ cup corn flour (harina de maíz)

IF YOU DRIVE TWENTY MILES south of my border hometown, Tijuana, you hit Rosarito, a beach town really popular with young Americans for its nightclubs (and Mexico's lower drinking age). Unknown to most of the tourists though, is the *callejón del tamal,* a small strip just north of Rosarito with about fifteen different corn tamal stalls. You go, eat as many as you can from the different vendors, then pick your fave!

Tamales can take a couple of days to make if you're using an intricate filling. In this easy recipe, the masa ingredients are all mixed in a bowl and just spread on dried corn husks, making for softer tamales with a shorter prep time. Traditionally, tamales are made with lard, but in this recipe (and in a lot of traditional ones) butter is used instead to bind the ingredients. I'm often asked what the best substitute is for lard or butter when making a tamal. My answer? Make enchiladas instead.

1 Soak the corn husks for 30 minutes in cold water.

2 Puree the corn kernels in a blender or food processor until smooth.

3 In the bowl of an electric mixer, beat the butter and sugar until pale. Mix in the egg, salt, and baking powder. Add half of the corn flour and mix until fully incorporated. Add half of the pureed corn and mix well. Repeat with the remaining flour and pureed corn to make a loose dough. Let dough stand in the refrigerator overnight.

4 Position a corn husk vertically in front of you with the wide side closest to you. Spread 3 tablespoons of the dough all over the bottom half (wide side) of the corn husk, leaving about a 1-inch border on the left and right

(recipe continues)

sides and along the bottom. Pick up the 2 long sides of the corn husk and unite them. Roll them together in the same direction over the tamal. Fold down the empty top section of the corn husk and secure it by tying a thin strip of corn husk around the tamal (the top will be open). Repeat with the remaining corn husks until the dough is used up.

5 Create a tamal steamer by crumpling a large piece of aluminum foil into a ball the size of a large orange. Put the foil ball in the center of a large saucepan and arrange the tamales vertically, with open sides up, standing around it. You can stand tamales in front of each other; just make sure that the open end of each tamal is facing upward.

6 Pour in ½ inch of water. Cover tightly with a lid and bring to a boil. Lower the heat and simmer until the corn husks separate easily from the masa, about 1 hour.

7 Remove the tamales from the steamer and let cool for 5 minutes before serving in the husk.

NOTE Corn husks, the leafy outer covering of an ear of corn, can be purchased dried at Latin markets and some supermarkets. They need to be soaked in hot water for 30 minutes, or until they become soft and pliable so they can stand up to the long cooking time of tamales. Dry them with paper towels before using. People often ask me what a good substitution is. You could use banana leaves, but they're even harder to source and because they aren't porous like corn husks, tamales steamed in them come out greasy-looking to me (though some cooks actually prefer this!). Parchment paper can be used; just make sure to coat it with cooking spray first. I also recommend making your *tamal* masa not too loose in that case; otherwise you'll find it very difficult to enclose the masa in the parchment.

leftovers?

tamal and rajas casserole: Remove tamales from husks. Chop the tamales and arrange in a glass baking dish. Top with Mexican crema or sour cream, strips of roasted poblanos, and shredded Monterey Jack cheese, then broil until the cheese bubbles.

sweet corn tamales: Warm the tamales and top with a drizzle of sweetened condensed milk, some ground cinnamon, and raisins.

cinnamon PAN FRANCES

serves 6 to 8

3 large eggs

¾ cup whole milk

¼ cup Mexican crema or
heavy cream

1 tablespoon plus 2 teaspoons
ground cinnamon

1 tablespoon pure vanilla
extract

1 cup plus 1 teaspoon sugar

4 bolillo rolls (see Note, page
46), or 1 baguette, cut into
2 × 3-inch rectangles

4 tablespoons (½ stick)
unsalted butter, plus more
for serving

Maple syrup, warmed

JUST AS YOU NEVER THROW AWAY A STALE TORTILLA, there's always
something you can do with stale bread. Biting into this Mexican
version of French toast is like eating into a soft churro. Serve with
seasonal, fresh berries and plenty of maple syrup.

1 Whisk together the eggs, milk, crema, 2 teaspoons of
the cinnamon, the vanilla, and 1 teaspoon of the sugar.
Pour into a 9 × 13-inch glass baking dish. Add the
bread and turn to coat with the egg mixture. Cover
and let stand until the bread absorbs the egg mixture,
about 5 minutes.

2 Mix the remaining 1 cup sugar and 1 tablespoon
cinnamon on a plate.

3 Melt 2 tablespoons of the butter in a large heavy skillet
over medium heat. Add 4 bread slices and cook until
golden brown and warmed through, about 3 minutes
per side. Transfer the French toast to the plate with the
cinnamon sugar and turn to coat. Repeat, working in
3 more batches, with the remaining butter and bread.

4 Serve with maple syrup.

mexican chocolate–date FRITTERS

serves 6 to 8

THESE ARE SWEET ENOUGH TO HAVE FOR DESSERT, but I often eat them for breakfast. Either way, serve them with a fresh batch of Mexican hot chocolate so you can dunk these delights. They would be an impressive part of a Christmas Day breakfast, when dates and mandarins are in season.

1   Whisk together the flour, baking powder, tangerine zest, salt, chocolate, and dates in a large bowl. Whisk together the requesón, eggs, granulated sugar, and vanilla in another large bowl. Add the flour mixture and mix until well incorporated. The batter will be coarse.

2   Pour enough oil into a heavy medium saucepan to come halfway up the sides of the pan. Heat the oil to 350°F.

3   Working in batches, gently drop heaping tablespoons of batter in the oil and fry, turning occasionally, until deep golden in color, about 3 minutes. Transfer with a slotted spoon to paper towels to drain. Dust generously with confectioners' sugar. Serve with Mexican hot chocolate.

¾ **cup all-purpose flour**

2 **teaspoons baking powder**

1 **teaspoon grated tangerine zest**

¼ **teaspoon salt**

¼ **cup minced Mexican or bittersweet chocolate**

¼ **cup minced pitted dates**

1 **cup requesón or whole-milk ricotta**

2 **large eggs, lightly beaten**

2 **tablespoons granulated sugar**

1½ **teaspoons pure vanilla extract**

Vegetable oil, for frying

Confectioners' sugar, for dusting

drinks

a farmer's market has recently opened in Tijuana, and it's about a block away from the home where my grandparents used to live. On one of my last visits, I went to check it out and was so impressed with all the wonderful local and organic products as well as the artisanal cheeses and homemade jams and jellies. It was a really hot day, so what I remember the most is the *agua fresca de chia y limón* (Chia Lemonade; page 212). I've always known about using chia seeds in drinks, but the truth is I'd never actually tasted them in one! It was positively the most refreshing, addictive, and delicious agua fresca I'd ever had. Many of the drinks in this chapter are inspired by finds such as this.

And while everybody knows that if I'm eating a taco at a stand in Tijuana, I'm drinking an orange soda, when my family comes over to the house on Christmas, soda is absolutely, positively unacceptable. They walk into the house, and before they even say hello, they ask, "Where's the Warm Winter Punch?" Drinks like this (page 208) can make an evening more memorable and so much more fun, especially if they're spiked! So invite some friends, make a few appetizers, and surprise your guests with a Mexican Hot Chocolate (page 207) for dessert. *Salud* everybody!

spicy CLAMATO AND BEER

FOUND ALL ACROSS MEXICO, these spicy cocktails are supposed to cure a hangover, and are often served with minced clams at the bottom to nibble on. The celery-stick garnish is also traditional. Made with beer, they're like gentle Mexican bloody Marys!

1 Put some salt on a small plate. Using the lime wedge, moisten the rims of 2 beer mugs. Invert the mugs into the salt to coat the rims.

2 Combine the lime juice, clam juice, tomato juice, and hot sauce in a medium bowl. Divide between the prepared beer mugs. Add ice to each and then pour 1 beer into each mug. Garnish each with a celery stick and serve.

serves 2

Salt

½ lime wedge

¼ cup fresh lime juice

¼ cup bottled clam juice

3 cups bottled tomato juice

¾ teaspoon hot sauce

Ice cubes

2 (12-ounce) cans of light beer

2 celery sticks

cucumber MARTINI

serves 4 to 6

CUCUMBER MARTINIS ARE NOW POPULAR in bars all over Mexico, along with many other fruit-based martinis like mango, tamarind, and guava. Mellow, crisp vodka pairs nicely with fresh cucumber; for the rim, try to get your hands on some chile-lime powder (Tajin is my favorite brand), found in the candy section of Mexican markets. Sometimes the rim is coated with a mixture of salt, sugar, and powdered chile, but ground dried chile often overpowers the fresh flavor of the martini. The dehydrated lime juice in the chile-lime powder brings out the bright taste of the cucumber.

¼ cup sugar

Chile-lime powder or salt

½ lime, cut into wedges

2 large cucumbers, peeled and thinly sliced (reserve 4 to 6 slices for garnish)

3 tablespoons fresh lime juice

4 cups cold water

2 ounces (¼ cup) vodka

Ice cubes

1 In small saucepan, bring ¼ cup of water and sugar to a boil over medium high-heat. Simmer until the sugar has dissolved completely, 8 minutes. Set the simple syrup aside to cool.

2 Put the chile-lime powder on a small plate. Using the lime wedge, moisten the rims of the martini glasses. Invert the martini glasses into the chile-lime powder to coat the rims.

3 In a blender, puree the simple syrup, cucumber, lime juice, and cold water until smooth. Strain the mixture into a pitcher. Add the vodka and mix well.

4 For each drink, fill a cocktail shaker with ice and add about 1 cup of the cucumber mixture. Shake well, then strain into a prepared glass. Garnish each glass with a cucumber slice and serve.

pineapple-vanilla AGUA FRESCA

2 cups roughly chopped fresh pineapple

3 cups cold water

½ teaspoon pure vanilla extract

3 tablespoons sugar, or to taste

Ice cubes

AGUA FRESCA MEANS "FRESH WATER," which is exactly what this drink is—super fresh. In Mexico, you can find aguas frescas made with every single fruit; the trick is to always use fruit that's in season so you don't have to add too much sugar. I love the combination of tart pineapple and fragrant vanilla, and when I make this for my friends, I always put a pitcher on the table along with a bottle of rum in case somebody needs a little splash of happiness in the agua fresca.

1 Put the pineapple, cold water, vanilla, and sugar in a blender and process until smooth.

2 Strain into a pitcher, pressing on the solids to extract all the liquid; discard the solids. Add more sugar, if necessary. Serve chilled over ice.

mexican HOT CHOCOLATE

BUY A DISK OF MEXICAN CHOCOLATE, dissolve it in milk, and you're done. You can substitute bittersweet chocolate with ground cinnamon and a few drops of almond extract, but you won't get the fuller texture you get from the unrefined sugar in Mexican chocolate bars. A Mexican hot chocolate frother, known as a *molinillo,* will give you the proper foamy consistency, but I've found that rolling a whisk between the palms of your hand will give you the same effect. If you happen to have an immersion blender, that will also do the trick; you just won't burn off any calories!

makes 4 cups

4 cups whole milk

1 (3.1-ounce) disk Mexican chocolate

Bring the milk to a simmer in a large heavy saucepan over medium-high heat. Add the chocolate, reduce the heat to medium-low, and simmer for 10 minutes, whisking constantly to develop froth and completely melt the chocolate. Serve immediately.

warm winter PUNCH

3½ cups apple juice

1 (3-inch) cinnamon stick

2 tablespoons sugar

2 cups chopped dried fruit
(any assortment)

8 ounces (1 cup) reposado
tequila

MY MOM USED TO MAKE THIS DRINK, known as a *ponche caliente*, during the holiday season. She'd always make two batches, one with tequila for the grownups and one without for the little ones. Either way, the smell of cinnamon and warm apple cider would fill the air and you knew Christmas was close. You certainly want the dried fruit to soften a little and impart some flavor, but you don't want it to get mushy so don't let it sit in the punch too long.

1 Combine the apple juice and cinnamon in a heavy medium saucepan. Bring to a boil, reduce the heat, and simmer for 10 minutes. Remove the cinnamon stick.

2 Stir in the sugar, dried fruit, and tequila. Serve warm.

chocolate MARGARITA

THERE ARE VARIOUS VERSIONS of how this cocktail came to be, but who really cares? You've got a whole bunch of chocolate and just as much tequila—two of Mexico's most relevant culinary contributions—in a glass of deliciousness. The drink is relatively sweet, as it should be with three different kinds of chocolate, so serve this more as a dessert than an apéritif. Mexican Chocolate–Date Fritters (page 199) would be a great pairing.

2 tablespoons finely chopped Mexican or bittersweet chocolate, for the glasses

½ cup chocolate syrup, plus more for the glasses

8 ounces (1 cup) añejo tequila

4 ounces (½ cup) chocolate liqueur

2.6 ounces (⅓ cup) orange liqueur, such as Triple Sec

⅓ cup heavy cream

1 teaspoon almond extract

1 teaspoon ground cinnamon

Ice cubes

1 Put the chocolate on a small plate. Moisten the rims of 4 cocktail glasses (martini or margarita) with chocolate syrup. Invert the glasses into the chocolate to coat the rims.

2 Whisk together the chocolate syrup, tequila, chocolate liqueur, orange liqueur, heavy cream, almond extract, and ground cinnamon in a pitcher.

3 For each drink, fill a cocktail shaker with ice and add about ¾ cup of the chocolate mixture. Shake well, then strain into a prepared glass, and serve.

chia LEMONADE

2 tablespoons chia seeds

5 cups cold water

½ cup sugar

1 cup fresh lime juice

CHIA SEEDS ARE NATIVE TO MEXICO AND CENTRAL AMERICA, and can be found in almost every supermarket or health store. These healthy little seeds are a great source of omega-3s and fiber, and they add a nice texture and fresh flavor to lemonade.

1 In a medium bowl, mix the chia seeds with 1 cup of cold water. Let stand for 15 minutes. Drain and rinse the seeds.

2 Mix the remaining 4 cups cold water and the sugar in a medium pitcher, stirring until the sugar dissolves. Add the lime juice and stir to combine. Mix in the chia seeds and serve cold.

OATMEAL **horchata**

serves 4

THIS IS A HEALTHY VERSION of a Mexican *horchata de arroz,* which is usually made with rice. Using the most nutritious of the cereal grasses, this horchata is often Fausto's breakfast, along with some fresh fruit and a slice of whole-grain toast.

1 In a large pitcher, soak the oats and cinnamon in the cold water for 30 minutes.

2 Blend the mixture (including the cinnamon) in a blender until smooth. Strain and sweeten with sugar to taste. Serve well chilled or over ice.

1 cup old-fashioned rolled oats

1 (3-inch) cinnamon stick, broken into tiny pieces

4 cups cold water

Sugar or agave nectar

Ice cubes

leftovers?

horchata raspado or granita: Pour the horchata into a glass baking dish and pop it in the freezer. Scrape with a fork every 30 minutes until frozen, for a delicious and refreshing raspado.

mexican piña colada: Combine equal parts Oatmeal Horchata and pineapple juice with some ice cubes in a blender. Add coconut rum for the grownups.

horchata gelatin: Mix in unflavored gelatin according to package directions to set the horchata mixture in a Bundt pan in the refrigerator (you need about 2 cups liquid and a ¼-ounce envelope or gelatin). Unmold and serve with drizzled condensed milk and fresh fruit.

citrus SPRITZER

¼ **cup water**

¼ **cup agave nectar**

Juice of 1 grapefruit

Juice of 2 navel oranges

Juice of 2 tangerines

Juice of 2 lemons

3 cups sparkling water

IN MEXICO WE HAVE A DRINK CALLED A *NARANJADA*, which is simply fresh orange juice and either flat or sparkling water with a little sugar. I make it all the time, but I usually add any citrus that I have available for more flavor and freshness.

1 Over medium-high heat, bring the water and agave to a boil. Once the mixture comes to a boil, remove it from heat. Let syrup cool.

2 Combine the grapefruit, orange, tangerine, and lemon juices in a pitcher. Stir in the syrup and then the sparkling water. Serve cold or over ice.

menus

MOTHER'S DAY BRUNCH
Shrimp and Avocado Salad, 25

Chicken and Tomatillo Enchilada Gratin, 184

Crimini Mushrooms Stuffed with Chard, 131

Pineapple-Cajeta Empanadas, 164

Citrus Spritzer, 214

MEXICAN GRILL PARTY
Panela Cheese Drenched in Chipotle Cream, 24

Creamy Mexican Corn, 118

Burgers al Pastor, 72

The 2 A.M. Hot Dog, 82

Spicy Clamato and Beer, 203

Bananas Tequila Foster, 166

CINCO DE MAYO
Chicken Flautas, 28

Skirt Steak Quesadillas, 31

Homemade Queso Fresco with Jalapeño and Cilantro, 20

Arroz Rojo, 132

Cucumber Martini, 205

DAY OF THE DEAD CELEBRATION
Sweet Ancho Chiles in Black Bean Salsa, 97

Beef Pozole, 58

Garlicky Buttered Baja Shrimp, 93

Coconut Flan, 159

Warm Winter Punch, 208

THANKSGIVING
Crimini Mushrooms Stuffed with Chard, 131

Spiced Turkey Breast with Chocolate Pasilla Sauce, 88

Acorn Squash and Roasted Garlic Mash, 122

Yukon Potato, Poblano, and Corn Gratin, 128

Caramelized Yams with Marshmallow and Streusel, 136

Mexican Chocolate Pecan Pie, 163

HEALTHY MEXICAN
Chayote with Yogurt Dip, 124

Roasted Cherry Tomato Soup, 64

Taco Light, 45

Red and White Kidney Bean Salad, 109

Figs in Red Wine and Honey, 167

CHRISTMAS BREAKFAST

Oven-Roasted Poblano and
Egg Casseroles, 181

Opened-Faced Bean and Cheese
Sandwiches with Roasted Apple
and Tomatillo Salsa, 191

Mexican Chocolate–Date Fritters, 199

Mexican Hot Chocolate, 207

DÍA DEL NIÑO

Extra-Cheesy Mex Mac 'N Cheese, 101

Braised Marinated Skirt Steak Burritos, 40

Corn and Zucchini Sauté, 120

Mexican Chocolate Bread Pudding, 160

TACO STAND

Homemade Flour Tortillas, 35

Chicken in Easy Adobo, 85

Slow-Cooked Carnitas Tacos, 36

Foil-Wrapped Onions, 135

Pecan and Chile de Árbol Salsa, 144

APRÈS SKI LUNCH

Queso Fundido with Chorizo, 19

Roasted Butternut Squash Salad with
Tangerine-Rosemary Vinaigrette, 114

Creamy Pinto Bean Soup, 61

Torta de Milanesa, 48

Banana and Cajeta Layered Crepes, 174

MEXICAN INDEPENDENCE DAY

Steamed Clams with Chorizo and Tequila, 21

Victor's Caesar Salad, 111

Stuffed Poblanos with Walnut Sauce, 75

Requesón Cheesecake, 168

DULCE DELIGHTS

Requesón Cheesecake, 168

Chocolate-Mint Pots de Crème, 171

Banana and Cajeta Layered Crepes, 174

Figs in Red Wine and Honey, 167

gracias

I get a phone call every day at around 7:45 A.M. I pick up the phone and I get the same question: *"Cuanto me quieres?"* (How much do you love me?) And every morning I answer with the same *"De aquí a jupiter."* (From here to Jupiter.) Then my father asks me if I need any money (I always say no, thank you), and the last question is "When are you coming to Tijuana?" I adore you, Dad. I walk through life with a huge safety net under me. I take enormous leaps with the assurance that if I fall you will always be there to catch me. Thank you.

To my mom, I have never looked more like you than in the photographs in this book. I can only hope it is also a reflection of who I am becoming on the inside as well. I miss you, but I know you're here.

To Cari, *mi red,* what would I do without you? If Dad is the safety net, you're my partner on the trapeze. I love you, sis. You, Isa, Danskin, and Gabs brighten up my life. Ray, thanks for putting up with my sister and inviting me and Fau to lunch all those family Sundays.

To Toño, *hermano,* tough on the outside, soft as a Mexican marshmallow on the inside. The days I spend with you, Lisa, Luís To, Pa, David, and Vicky are some of my happiest.

To Vivs, what would I do without you?

To Vale, I told you in my first book it was only the beginning, and look at us now!

To Janet, there is nothing more valuable than the peace of mind that comes from leaving Fau with someone I trust. Fau and I both appreciate you so much. Plus you can cook!

To my *tía* Marcela, you are my teacher and best friend.

To the boys of WME—Philip Button, Mark Mullet, Jon

Rosen, and Eric Lupfer—thank you for your guidance, hard work, and belief in me.

To Raúl, how far we've come since that first meeting in Miami when I was so nervous you offered me some tequila . . . *Eres una bala y me siento afortunada de que has estado con migo todo el camino.*

To my *familia* at The Door—Charlie Dougiello, Caroline Bubnis, and Lois Najarian—you guys put this Tijuana girl on the map.

To my Food Network family—Bob Tuschman, Susie Fogelson, Amanda Melnick, Irika Slavin, Lauren Mueller, Sharon DeGier, Karen Berrios, Harriet Siew, Allison Page, and Jill Novatt—thank you all for this wonderful opportunity.

To my editor at Clarkson Potter/Random House, Rica Allannic, not only for your flawless editing but for those conversations about being working moms of six-year-old little boys. You've saved me *mucho dinero* of therapy.

To the whole Clarkson Potter team—Lauren Shakely, Doris Cooper, Ashley Phillips, Kate Tyler, Jill Browning, Donna Passannante, Allison Malec, Jane Treuhaft, Stephanie Huntwork, Megan McLaughlin, Mark McCauslin, and Kim Tyner—thank you for your work on this book.

To my photographer, Jen Martiné, for making my food look the best it's ever looked.

To my prop stylist, Dani, I knew we were going to be just fine when I arrived at the studio and I wanted to steal all the props for my house. What exquisite taste you have!

To my food stylist, Karen Shinto, it's like you grew up in Mexico with these authentic, perfect, and gorgeous platings.

To Enrique Castillo and Susana Navarrete for the flawless smoky eye and perfect beachy wave. I feel I have magical powers when I'm all made up by either of you.

To Andrea Bolaños for the beautiful custom-made jewelry.

To my producers at Hip Entertainment—Doug and Beatriz Acevedo-Greiff. We've cooked in Spanish, we've cooked in

English, *and* our kids hang out. Thank you for pushing for me from day one.

To the whole *Mexican Made Easy* TV crew. I so appreciate how you invest heart and soul to each of your responsibilities.

To my Facebook friends and Twitter followers; I read every single comment and appreciate every word of support.

To my friends whom have known me for at least a couple decades—you know who you are—for always being there. I've missed so many birthdays and baby showers, and yet your support is still unwavering.

To my dog, Yogo, because this is my cookbook and I can thank whomever I want. He's been with me for twelve years and I love him as much as everybody on this page.

To all those unknown chefs and cooks in all of the *taquerías, cenadurías,* and *restaurantes* all across Mexico who have so inspired me. I work so hard everyday to make sure I give Mexican cuisine the respect it deserves.

To my beloved hometown, Tijuana, so misunderstood, yet exploding with potential, talent, and heart. I am who I am for having spent the first thirty years of my life there.

And last and most important, to my Fausto, the love of my life, my partner in crime, my travel buddy. You were born and I was born. You make me a better person every day. We're a team, little one. Your dad and I are the luckiest parents in the world. So many more trips are coming, so many more restaurants, so many more adventures that I look forward to with so much more excitement because I know you'll be there with me. Such a huge, huge world, and I'm dying to see it with you. All this cooking stuff is fabulous, but being your mom is what fills my heart with joy every single day.

It only took ten years for me to get on Food Network, and every single one of you had something to do with the journey that brought me to this show and book. *Gracias. Los quiero y hasta la próxima . . .*

index

Note: Page references in *italics* indicate photographs